*How to use your physical and
emotional ability to
overcome your problems
and reach your goals*

How to use your physical and emotional ability to overcome your problems and reach your goals

EUGENE J. BENGE

DOW JONES-IRWIN   Homewood, Illinois   60430

First Printing, January 1977

ISBN 0-87094-128-3
Library of Congress Catalog Card No. 76-13082
Printed in the United States of America

Preface

The purpose of this book is to explain simply and directly what modern science knows about our physical and emotional ability to overcome our problems and reach our goals. It has been my business for over 30 years to observe and explain what factors account for success and achievement. What is in this book represents what I have learned from hundreds of executives, doctors, teachers, ministers, and happy people.

In this book you will discover how to overcome stress and master your emotions. The section on diet and exercise explains how to increase your energy level and have more pep. There are specific suggestions and exercises to help you recognize and take advantage of your strengths and overcome your weaknesses.

This book is to be used as a stepping stone to a richer, fuller, and more exciting life.

I have seen these methods work and change the lives of thousands of people. All of us have the ability to change. All of us have the opportunity to use what we have been born with and what we have been taught. All of us can take advantage of what this book explains. Read it and I know you will agree.

December 1976   EUGENE J. BENGE

Contents

Great knowledge is available to you. Inertia. Where do you now stand?
Your heredity. Your childhood. Health and energy. Character.
Patience, my friend. Your experience. Your self-image. False self-
images. Don't sell yourself short. Feel insecure? Hidden life power.
Changing attitudes toward work. Are you a conformist? Some day I'll
be happy.

The physical cause first. Length of life increasing. How to live a long
time. Your health—work at it. Attack each minor ailment. So you're
overweight! Laughter—good exercise. Are you a type "A" person?
Look—to your eyes. The sentries of health. Noise. Arthritis, anyone?
Cancer—No. 1 killer. Want to avoid the No. 2 killer? Diabetes—killer
No. 3. Are you a slave to the weather? Get an annual checkup.
Allergies. Self-appraisal.

Exercise. So, you have a desk job. How about jogging? Efficient use of
muscles. Some exercise fallacies. Two kinds of fatigue. Command
muscles to relax. If you're a type "A" person. Gain an extra hour every

day. Some sleep hints. Play—for your health. Your posture. Some don't know how to walk.

Vocabulary. Simple ways to strengthen your vocabulary. Reasoning. How to improve your reasoning powers. Space perception. Improving your space perception. Improve your reading speed. College, everyone?

List of illustrations

Introduction

Are you wearing yourself out trotting on the treadmill to oblivion? Are you afraid to make a decisive break with a troubled, defeated past? If it's any comfort to you—and I hope it won't be—you have lots of company. World-wide, millions of harried men and women entertain similar self-doubts.

Your very apprehension, however, can become a springboard to greater health, security, and, above all, happiness. This book can chart the passage, but you're the one who must make the voyage.

The ancient Greeks told the story of Atalanta, the fleet-footed virgin huntress who agreed to marry any young man who could defeat her in a foot race—but he would have to forfeit his life if he failed. Alas, many did. Finally, a challenger came along who could not run faster, but who had three golden apples given him by Aphrodite. As Atalanta drew away from him, he tossed golden apples ahead of her. She stopped to pick them up—and so lost the race.

Life throws many shining golden apples ahead of you and me: diversions, excuses, procrastination, laziness, grumbling, impractical dreams. If we stop for them, we'll surely lose life's race to those who just keep running.

In an ancient village there was an old man who was considered very wise. A brash youth sought to confound him by saying, "I hold in my hand a small bird. Tell me, Wise One, is he dead or alive?" If the old man said "dead," the young man would allow the bird to fly away. If "alive," he'd crush the bird. In either event, the wise man would be proved wrong. But the old one simply said to the youth, "As thou wilt, my son."

Your destiny rests in *your* hands. You can do with it as thou wilt.

The greatest enemy of your future success is the person you have let yourself become. You cannot hope to improve yourself if you continue your present living habits and attitudes. Admittedly it is not easy to break the chains of habits which enslave you, but that is what I'm asking you to do.

What is truly known about the factors of success? Will those known factors apply to success in the future? These are complex, challenging questions. For one thing, there are many kinds of success—money, security, status, fame, accomplishment, serenity, service to others, friendship and love, to name some that come quickly to mind.

The success-contributing factors spelled out in this book underlie almost any kind of success. The factors tend to be mutually supportive. Each one augments the others, and their combined effect is multiplicative, not additive. Good health makes possible high energy, which contributes to accomplishment, yielding satisfaction that helps emotional balance, and so on.

In a relay race there are usually four runners. Each one hands the baton on to the next; the final runner is generally the best.

Your life can be likened to such a race. Runner One is you for the first six years of your life. Runner Two is you through your school days. Runner Three is your adulthood to this day. This book hands the baton to you, Runner Four. How fast will you go to finish the race?

Let me change the metaphor. In Switzerland there are "VITA-Parcours," health-walking paths. They offer 20 different calisthenic stations, with a chance to rest after each one. You may spend a challenging hour to complete the exercise rounds; it's fun, and leaves you feeling full of pep.

You can consider the chapters of this book as "stations" on your way to a permanently higher success level.

Yes, it's true: by whatever criterion of success you use, only small percentages of folks achieve it. Not many capture wealth, fame, or inner serenity—and some who realize one, such as wealth, may fail miserably in another, such as serenity. And vice versa.

Dr. Walter Dill Scott, psychologist and a former professor of mine, used to tell us that we could increase our total effectiveness 50 percent *within a few weeks,* if we really wanted to—if we *really wanted to!*

Another renowned psychologist, William James, wrote: "We are only half awake—making use of a small part of our physical and mental resources. The human individual . . . possesses powers of various sorts which he habitually fails to use."

In the long run, emotional tranquility must be considered the pinnacle of success. Without it, other kinds of success are hollow. We *can* become much more than we now are. Strive for it! You can do it!

1
Take stock of your assets

You already possess great capacity for a full and rewarding life. Some portion of this capacity exists in hidden talents which you scarcely know you possess, and in great emotional power which you may rarely have used *constructively*.

Contrariwise, you probably have some physical, mental, or emotional handicaps which must either be accepted, or overcome.

> A successful business owner will periodically appraise his property, machinery, tools, raw materials, work in process, finished goods, and cash. He will match the value of these items against his obligations to stockholders, vendors, banks, and tax collectors. The results will appear on his balance sheet as his net worth.

Your "balance sheet" will provide a frame of reference for many resolves and decisions you make as you read this book. Fortunately, you have the power to profit from your past mistakes, if you will but use it. In this chapter you will take an inventory of both your assets and your liabilities.

Maybe secretly you suspect that you are just a run-of-the-mine person, with no unusual talents or personality. Yet history tells us that so-called ordinary people can make extraordinary effort, breaking the fetters that bind their lives.

Conversely, you may feel confident that you possess certain talents well above average. If this is your case, you need to seek out situations which will utilize those talents.

In either case, your candid self-appraisal should inventory the existing building blocks of your near-term life. Based on them, you construct your long-term life.

GREAT KNOWLEDGE IS AVAILABLE TO YOU

I have some good news and some bad news for you. First, the bad news: In the turbulent, change-charged period ahead, millions of hope-filled Americans will unwind their lives as frustrated failures.

Now for the good news: You don't have to be one of them!

In all fields of human endeavor much more is known than is practiced. Scientific discoveries lie fallow for 10, 20, 30 years before they are translated into useful products, services, institutions, beliefs, actions. Nowhere is this lag more in evidence than in the broad field of human development. Research in medicine and in sociology, psychology, and other social sciences has produced vast knowledge which can help you avoid many pitfalls and spur your progress.

Unfortunately, most of this useful knowledge lies dormant in hundreds of scattered sources which you might never encounter. This book endeavors to give you up-to-date information on how you can develop yourself physically, mentally, socially and emotionally—further, how you can coordinate this information to make a joyful life and a self-reliant living.

Obviously, these benign resultants won't happen just because you read this—or any other—book. You must want to change—to improve yourself—to achieve greater peace of mind—to face the future with faith and courage. The wisdom of the human race is at your command, if you will but use it. Will you?

A friend told me this story:

> At final exams just before the Christmas holidays, "What Causes Depressions?" was the one and only question in an economics course. One student, who had only an hour to plane time, wrote, "God only knows. Merry Christmas, professor." Back from the holidays, his graded paper was returned to him with the notation, "God gets 100. You get 0. Happy New Year."

Some individuals are so cocksure of themselves that they never bother to learn what others before them have discovered. They secretly pride themselves that they are self-made men. A few will ruefully admit that they're the product of unskilled labor, that if they had it to do over again, they'd get help. Still others brag about being self-made—and how they love their maker!

The unvarnished truth is that you are the result of heredity, environment, and self-determination. You can do nothing about your heredity, nor about your past environment. But you *can* alter or change your future environment, and further can take complete charge of your future thought and action. To do so you must overcome your inertia and get all the help you can muster.

INERTIA

To the physicist, the term "inertia" means that a moving mass will continue on its present course unless that is altered by some impinging force. In the case of human beings that force is likely to be environment or economics. However—happy day—it can be *self-generated*. You can mold your future by wise use of the present. That present, as it now stands, consists of accumulated bits of the past, but starting today you can add new pieces for your future. Bear in mind the Chinese proverb that "The journey of a thousand miles begins with the first step." Ruts are comfortable, but until you climb out of them you don't go anywhere.

WHERE DO YOU NOW STAND?

To plan your future you need first to understand your past and present. Even if you would be content to contemplate your future as merely a continuation of the present, the fast-changing world will deny you this luxury. For you, today is the best of times, or the worst of times—as *you* view it. The fact that you are reading this book suggests that you are not content with the present direction of your life; that you long to become a superior person; that you are open to new ideas which will help you develop physically, mentally, socially and emotionally.

To aid your self-understanding, this book will present you with a number of self-analysis scales, similar to the one shown in Figure 1. Complete each scale thoughtfully. Neither pat yourself on the back

FIGURE 1
What am I, really?

In each of the ten lines below, check the block which comes closest to your self-appraisal. If you can't decide between two blocks, check the narrow space between them. Be honest, but not harsh with yourself!

General attribute	*2*	*3*	*4*	*5*	*6*	*7*	*8*	*9*	*10*
Health	My health is very poor		I have too many physical problems		I'm about average in health		I'm rarely ill		I enjoy outstanding health
Energy	I get exhausted under pressure		I fatigue too easily		Occasionally I feel energetic		Frequent spurts of energy		I rarely feel tired
Memory	I admit it's very bad		Am often forgetful		I'm poor at remembering names		I use notes and ticklers to help my memory		Friends admire my memory
Mental development	I don't believe I'm a "brain"		I've always been slow mentally		About average, I guess		I've developed my mental powers		I have a very high I.Q.
Social development	I prefer being alone		I'm a shy person		I wish I could mix better		I like to be with small groups		I love hilarious groups
Leadership	Usually I do what others direct		I dislike the limelight		I'll lead when necessary		I like to lead in a few areas		I'm usually made the leader
Emotional maturity	I "blow my top" readily		I'm frequently jittery		Sometimes I feel depressed		I've adjusted to my circumstances		Under pressure, I maintain poise
Environment	Is extremely aggravating		I'd like to escape it		Occasionally it's annoying		My surroundings are peaceful		My environment is stimulating
Accomplishments	Afraid I'm a failure		I haven't done much with my life		I've done enough to get by		I'm proud of some of my achievements		I've already accomplished a lot for my age
Ambition	I don't believe I have any		I no longer care much		I'm still striving for a few things		I'm more ambitious than most people		I'm driven by consuming ambition

nor kick yourself lower down; just be impartially honest. Fill out
Figure 1 *now*.

YOUR HEREDITY

Heredity versus environment is an old argument, with proponents on either side. Some adults with seemingly poor heredity and
environment do well financially or make important contributions
to mankind. Others from the same or similar backgrounds waste
their lives in trivia or become criminals. Per contra, not all children
from highly successful lineage and culturally advantaged backgrounds make successes of their lives, although the odds are in
their favor.

These statements mean that your success, however you define it,
lies pretty much in your own hands. (A friend of mine says that he
was a strong believer in heredity until he saw the strange antics of
his teenage son.) Few of us ever approach the limits of our capacity. Instead, we are what we learn to do and be, not what our
forebears imposed on us, seldom considering that we have far more
potential than we are using.

YOUR CHILDHOOD

Psychiatrists believe that your childhood plays an important part
in molding your character and in determining how you will react
to others. Some important childhood influences are: (1) what the
child wants versus what he gets, and (2) parental (and sibling)
attention, ranging through hostility, indifference, and security, to
affection. Figure 2 suggests possible outcomes from varying combinations of these two influences. As an exercise, you are invited
to study this figure. You may not agree with it. If not, what personality characteristics would you predict from the 16 combinations?

Do you think back fondly about your parents? Were they or
your brothers or sisters strong achievers? Was your home life peaceful most of the time? Were you allowed to think for yourself, to
try things on your own? Were you challenged and encouraged? All
such influences are favorable—but even if you answer no *to all of
them,* you can still surmount the negative effects they may have
had on you in your formative years.

FIGURE 2
Personality traits resulting from various home attitudes

Child	Attitude in home			
	Hostility	Indifference	Security	Affection
Wants and gets	Ruthless	"I'll show everyone I'm important"	Accepts security as a matter of course	Creative
Wants are denied	Radical	Hard worker	Seeks greater security	Mature, hard-driving
Does not want but is forced	Rebel	Cynical	Indifferent to security	Acceptant, unambitious
Does not want and is let alone	Withdrawn	Unambitious	Insecure	Sweet nonentity

Where would you place yourself in this figure?

Believe that your life has not been foreordained by your heredity and childhood. Even if your younger life was grim, understanding it can help you rise above its negative influence, while taking advantage of any positive aspects in it.

How much schooling have you had, whether in childhood or later? Education gives you a distinct advantage, especially if it is specific to your career path. Because of rapid business and social change, you should think in terms of life-long learning, and take additional study each year. (This area of your development will be considered in later chapters.) Advanced education only facilitates success, however; it does not guarantee it.

HEALTH AND ENERGY

Health and energy are separate concepts, although closely inter-related. At all ages, but particularly in your later years, health is basic to accomplishment. Whereas health is largely static, energy is dynamic.

We shall see later that poor health can cause a loss of energy, which detracts from mental effectiveness, arousing negative emotions which make poor health even worse.

Some years ago, I knew a happily married couple, both fine people and financially secure. He developed diabetes about the same time his wife was suffering from severe spinal arthritis. Each one introverted, felt sorry for him or herself. They ceased living for each other's happiness, finally divorced. Living apart solved neither one's physical problem, indeed aggravated it. Knowing these two as I did, I am convinced that if they had stayed together, had extroverted to help each other they would still be married and both happier than they are in their separate existences.

The analogy of a human being to an automobile has frequently been made. The various parts of an automobile, scattered over a plant, have little utility. Even when they are assembled, they are still inert. But give the completed machine both gasoline and electricity, and you have a powerful, ongoing piece of equipment.

So with you. Your body is like the assembled automobile. Fail to exercise some of its mental and physical parts and they will rust. Give it power from diet, ductless glands, and emotional balance, spark it with goals and other motivation—and you too will become a powerful, ongoing specimen of humanity.

CHARACTER

In self-examining your character development to date, realize that you may be looking at yourself through rose-tinted glasses.

Some years ago I taught night classes at Temple University in Philadelphia. As each school year closed, I asked each student to rank all members of his class (including himself) on ten traits (friendliness, intelligence, dominance, perseverance, etc.).

All ranks were converted to 1 to 100 scale (percentiles), so that the average would be 50, regardless of trait. The average of all *self*-ranks was 76, which meant that most students thought considerably better of themselves than did their fellow classmates.

Character has variously been defined as: (1) what you do when no one is looking over your shoulder; (2) what's left when you've lost everything; (3) how you treat social inferiors, servants or subordinates; (4) your treatment of people who can neither harm nor help you. The philosopher observes that how you play the game will reveal some of your character; how you lose at times will show all of it.

An early book in the field of psychology was titled *Character and Temperament,* by Dr. Joseph Jastrow. It contended that these two traits—character and temperament—were basic to human adjustment and success. No later findings have denied this thesis. So we can add one more definition to the four above: character is the bedrock of true success.

PATIENCE, MY FRIEND

Patience is a useful character trait. It is an essential ingredient of perseverance which is, however, a larger concept. Patience is for the moment; perseverance, for the long pull. Consider the "Patienscale" (I meant to spell it that way) in Figure 3 and score yourself on it.

Of course, you can be patient with your hands, impatient with

FIGURE 3
Patienscale

You can get an idea as to your patience by checking ten (and *only ten*) traits below which best describe you:

1. I'd enjoy refinishing a piece of furniture
2. Persistent questioning by young children annoys me
3. In most matters, I'm very patient
4. In controversy, I blow my top readily
5. In discussion, I let others finish what they have to say
6. I support most radical movements which seek social reform
7. Others are entitled to their opinions, so I rarely contradict
8. I open Christmas presents ahead of time
9. In an argument, I rarely raise my voice
10. People with slow hesitant speech annoy me
11. I believe social reform can only come gradually
12. In conversing, I frequently interrupt the other person
13. I'm very tolerant of children's antics and questioning
14. Prolonged mechanical work or handicraft irritates me
15. I await Christmas or birthday before opening my presents
16. When statements are wrong, I don't hesitate to contradict them
17. I'm tolerant of folks with slow or hesitant speech
18. Bad weather irritates me
19. I take bad weather in stride
20. I'm often accused of being impatient

To score yourself, subtract the number of even-numbered items from the odd-numbered and compare the result to this table:

Result		Significance
+ 8,	+ 10	Great patience
+ 4,	+ 6	Acceptable
0,	+ 2	Normal; Ho, hum
− 4,	− 2	Somewhat impatient
− 10, − 8,	− 6	Wow!

people; patient with your spouse, impatient with your children; patient with bad weather, impatient with your financial progress. What we're here considering is your usual stance toward obligations, people, and pressures.

Since patience contributes to serenity, it is conducive to longevity. However, carried to an extreme it can make one a subservient milquetoast on whom aggressive people will trample. In any situation, there is a point at which forebearance ceases to be a virtue.

YOUR EXPERIENCE

Your particular experience is unique, no one else can duplicate it exactly. It confers knowledge and skill upon you. It teaches you what to avoid. It enables you to earn a living, especially if you are more afraid of doing too little than too much.

Consider in what walks of life your experience will be most useful. Don't just await success in that line—push on to meet it halfway.

You own no credit card whereby you can avoid paying for your mistakes; soon or late the bill comes in. Perhaps some decision has gone sour. Instead of cursing your bad luck, or feeling guilty about the outcome, learn to learn from your mistake. If you profit by it, count that learning as an asset in your self-inventory.

YOUR SELF-IMAGE

Your self-image is the composite of your beliefs about yourself. Whether these beliefs are good or bad, true or false, you rarely question. Most of your self-generated actions, and many of your reactions, result from your self-image. Hence it is important to analyze your concept of self, to root out negative aspects in it, in order to build a better future based on its positive aspects.

As you awaken each day, ask yourself whether you will be a better person today than you were yesterday. If the answer is "probably not," there's always tomorrow for improvement of your self-image. Improvement today, however, is better.

In Figure 4 is a list of 25 beliefs about yourself which have probably contributed to your self-image. Rate each item by placing

FIGURE 4
Your self-image checklist

Compared with others of your acquaintance, what is your opinion of yourself as to your	Extremely low	Below average	Average	Above average	Very high
General health					
Energy level					
Memory for names					
Memory for faces					
Mathematical ability					
Vocabulary					
Reasoning powers					
Imagination					
Creativity					
Mechanical ingenuity					
Acceptance by others					
Dominance over others					
Public speaking ability					
Adjustment to present circumstances					
Calmness under stress					
Physical courage					
Perseverance					
Ability to make prompt decisions					
Ambition for more success					
Belief that you will win out					
Faith in your fellow man					
Faith in a God					
Freedom from fear of the future					
Freedom from resentment toward life					
Freedom from guilt burdens					
Number					

Total the checks in each rating column and multiply

Extremely low	X 0 =	0
Below average	X 1 =	
Average	X 2 =	
Above average	X 3 =	
Very high	X 4 =	
Total		

Refer your total to the following table for a generalized interpretation of your self-image

Total	*Interpretation*
0 to 30	You need to reconstruct your life
31 to 50	You have too many negatives
51 to 60	Your self-image is only normal
61 to 78	Good work, continue to improve
79 to 100	You have what it takes

a check mark in the appropriate column. (Don't skip any.) Then interpret the results.

Of additional value to you can be a careful study of all items you marked extremely low or below average. What steps should you take to raise these ratings?

Will you?

Does your self-image include acceptance of responsibility? If so, what kind and how much? In our national life, freedom and responsibility rise or fall together—and the same is true about you in your community, company, home, or personal life.

When you let your teenage son take the family car, you give him a certain freedom, and you hope for responsibility. Years ago, I knew a sales manager with a beautiful wife and two children who womanized as soon as he got to a distant city on a business trip; freedom, but irresponsibility. Many capable employees refuse jobs as foremen because they don't want the responsibility.

With responsibility goes accountability. The foreman must account to his superiors for his actions. In your community, company, home, do you accept responsibility? Are you prepared to account for your actions?

The strange part about responsiblity is that over your life, you may have to account for *failing* to accept it when opportunity presented itself.

FALSE SELF-IMAGES

Your self-image may differ from the way others see you.

> A successful businessman saw quite a lot of an actress, fell in love with her, and planned to ask her to marry him. Prudent man that he was, he first employed a private eye to report on her life. The detective summed up his report by saying "Excellent reputation. No past scandals. Impeccable friends. Only possible blemish is that lately she's been seeing a businessman of dubious reputation."

DON'T SELL YOURSELF SHORT

Speculators in the stock market may sell a stock "short"—stock which they do not own. They are betting that the value of that stock will go down so that they can later buy it at a lower price for delivery when demanded.

Don't sell yourself short with self-abasement or belittling remarks about your deficiencies. You are entitled to a place on this planet.

If you fail to act in accordance with your virtuous self-images, you will probably suffer guilt. At the other extreme, it is difficult to change your negative self-images—much easier to find proof or justification for your downbeat beliefs.

Here's a list of typical negative self-images:

I'm dumb	I'm sickly
I'm a poor speller	People don't like me
I'm poor at mathematics	I've failed my family
I can't get ahead in life	I can't speak in public
I can't remember names	I'm all thumbs at mechanics
I have a poor heredity	I'm afraid of _____
I can't sell	I'm unlucky
I'm a sinner	I'm very homely
I can't relax	I always get licked

Do any of these ring a bell with you? If so, attack the beliefs with actions which will enable you to change them to positive self-images.

FEEL INSECURE?

Your self-appraisal may make you realize that you secretly harbor some insecurities.

You are granted no permanent security in this life. When you accept that life can be hard, it starts to get easier for you. Over your lifetime, if you encounter the bad, you may then be able to appreciate the good.

You may be insecure because you're trying to be something you're not; or do something which, for you, is impossible; or please somebody who can't be pleased.

Maybe you're carrying some childhood illusions which, when shattered, leave you insecure. Here are some examples:

If I get a good education, I'll certainly be a success. (Sorry— there's more to success than book learning.)

All men are created equal. (Some are created more equal than others.)

Evil will always be punished. (How I wish this were true.)

If you lend money to people, they'll be grateful and pay you back as soon as they can. (Oh, yeh?)

For most of us, financial insecurity is the dreaded *bete noire,* but many who have achieved financial success fear that some economic cataclysm will take it away from them, or they suffer other insecurities, doubts, phobias.

At your command are a number of weapons to fight your insecurity. Courage, for example, knowledge-supported self-confidence, a healthier self-image and abundant opportunities. We shall get on good terms with these attributes as this book unfolds.

HIDDEN LIFE POWER

> Bet you never heard of a "tartigrade." It's a tiny, weird creature which looks like a fat crab designed by a group of uninhibited children. It can seem to be dead for scores of years, living without water, oxygen or heat—then come alive when it is moistened. Scientists call this phenomenal ability "crypto-biosis," which means hidden life.

You have many hidden abilities which can come to life under challenge, fear, or other motivation. Recently a widow said to me, "When Roger was alive, he took care of all financial problems—but it's amazing what I could do when I had to."

You don't have to await some emergency in your life to call upon your hidden reserves; you could be using them right now for your betterment. Don't just take my word for it; try it.

CHANGING ATTITUDES TOWARD WORK

Many of your present living habits have been developed because of work demands. Thus, you report for work at a specified time, expect to put in an eight-hour day, have a certain job expertise, accept the risk of unemployment, and so forth.

Attitudes toward work are changing. Flex-time allows leeway in reporting for work; some companies have instituted a four-day workweek of ten hours per day. Currently we witness longer vacations, more holidays, greater interest in leisure pursuits, less dedi-

FIGURE 5
Conformity test

Below are 96 jobs, arranged in groups of four. In each group, check the one occupation you would prefer over the other three. Consider only whether you would like that kind of work; ignore earning power or social status of the jobs; assume that you have the training for all of them.

Force yourself to make one choice—and only one—in each group by drawing a circle around the letter which precedes it.

D Sports writer A Pattern maker A Bond salesperson B Interpreter	A Insurance agent C Architect A Computer operator D Mining engineer	C Fiction writer A Tax assessor D Sailor B Politician	D Detective C Auto sales B Time study A Food store manager
C Locomotive engineer A Teacher, elementary D Auto designer A Teacher, mathematics	D Poet A Census clerk A Printer D War correspondent	A Bank clerk D Soldier, mercenary C Labor conciliator C Corporation lawyer	A Librarian B Bus driver C Landscape gardener D Band leader
C Real estate agent A Geologist B Astronomer D Aviator	B Farm crop forecaster A Truck repairer C Prosecuting attorney D Novelist	A Bricklayer B Hotel manager D Test pilot A Tax specialist	D Nightclub entertainer A Toolmaker B Science teacher A Bank teller
A Economist B Business forecaster D Explorer A Clergy	D Inventor C Auctioneer C Philosophy teacher A Building inspector	D Lion tamer A Radio repairer A Night watchman A Laboratory tester	A Punch press operator C Scout leader D Ad copy writer B Surveyor
B Statistician A Machinist D Sales manager C Bacteriologist	D Publicity agent C Magazine editor A Public accountant B Construction foreperson	B Poultry farmer A Hospital orderly A Hotel doorkeeper D Playwright	A Law clerk B Office manager A Cabinet maker D Trapese performer
A Photoengraver D Actor D Cartoonist A Cost estimator	B Editor, business A Cost clerk D Auto racer D Country doctor	B Social worker D Astronaut C Research chemist A Coal miner	A House painter D State trooper A Auditor A Auto mechanic

cation to the puritan ethic of thrift and work for work's sake, demands for insurance against unemployment, poorer adjustment to the regimentation of industry, boredom resulting from extreme subdivision of tasks, and alienation of employees from their ultimate bosses.

These and other characteristics of the post-industrial era inaugurated in the late '60s, may cause you to reevaluate the importance of some of your traits brought out by a study of your present assets. For some readers, a new career is in the offing. Others see opportunity because of less competition from their disinterested fellow workers.

Your study of your assets and liabilities should not exist in a vacuum. You must relate it to your career environment. In a South American jungle, survival knowledge would be more needed than computer capabilities; in a "think-tank" research group, just the reverse. So consider your self-evaluation in light of your milieu and the attitudes of others with whom you must work and socialize.

ARE YOU A CONFORMIST?

Some folks are strict conformists in their thoughts and actions, others are the exact opposite. In general, conformists keep society together, oppose change, and rarely get into trouble. The nonconformist is likely to be a radical, caring little for the opinions of others, toppling idols and frequently getting into hot water.

Most of us fall somewhere between these two extremes. Figure 5 is a simple test which will give you some idea as to where you stand. Whatever it suggests about you, the result is not to be viewed as either good or bad; society needs radicals to bring about change and conformists to maintain law and order. Evaluate the test finding from Figure 5 as to whether you believe it is valid, and if so, whether you should veer toward one direction or the other.

Total the number of each letter you have circled, enter below, multiply by the credits, and total the extensions.

	Number	Credit	Extension
A		× 1	
B		× 2	
C		× 3	
D		× 4	
	24		

Interpretation

74 to 96	Individualist; interest in unusual lines of work; possibly radical in thinking
54 to 73	Somewhat radical; tendency to nonconformity
44 to 53	Somewhat conservative; tendency to conform
24 to 43	Strong conformist; interest in orthodox jobs; possibly ultraconservative

Since this test considers jobs you'd like to do, it suggests occupational conformity, not necessarily social, political, religious or legalistic conformity. But it may tell you something about yourself that you may or may not have suspected as to your vocational life.

If conformity means that you are in a rut, climb out of it; if individualism means that, like Don Quixote, you are repeatedly tilting with windmills, maybe you should strive for a better adjustment to your situation.

SOME DAY I'LL BE HAPPY

... or healthy, wealthy, secure, at peace, have friends, master new knowledge, stop smoking, have fun. For many of us, that day eludes us; we make a living, but not a life.

But today is here. How you live it may determine your tomorrow.

Don't confuse worthy, distant goals with wholesome living today; you need both.

Today will never come again. It is wise to plan for your future, but equally wise to live the *now*. For your future, like a receding horizon, ever eludes you, but the present can be lived a day at a time. And the sum total of your todays will determine what you will be a year or a decade hence.

So, the self-appraisal advocated in this chapter really asks two questions: (1) What am I like now? (2) What would I like to be like in the years ahead?

Read on.

2

How healthy are you?

Health is an integral part of success—any kind of success. The wealthy financier who drives himself into a stomach ulcer is a dubious "success." The movie actress who has to dose herself with sleeping pills; the artist who suffers a spastic colon because he can't sell his paintings; the society matron who is neurotic because her husband ignores her—these are all examples of incomplete lives: maybe they're not failures but they sure are nonsuccesses.

Unbalanced diet; excessive use of tobacco, alcohol or drugs; insufficient exercise of the right kind; repeated or constant emotional strain may cause aging of your bodily organs at different rates. If you're 40 years old, you may have 50-year-old lungs, a 30-year-old heart, a 60-year-old liver—and you may be trying to live at the pace of a 20-year-old. Something's gotta give!

The time to reach for good health is in the morning or noon of your life, not wait until twilight when irreversible decay may have set in.

THE PHYSICAL CAUSE FIRST

The story is told of a man suffering from shortness of breath and heart palpitations. After examination, his physician regretfully gave him perhaps six months to live. So the man decided to live it up. He signed up for an extravagant world cruise, and bought expensive sport jackets and hand-tailored shirts, neck size 15. The tailor told him, "Your neck size is 16," but the man insisted on 15, said he'd always worn a 15. "O.K." said the tailor, "I'll make your shirts with a 15 neckband, but I must warn you that you'll suffer shortness of breath and palpitations of the heart."

So, before you consult your doctor about some ailment, ask yourself whether you are doing something wrong as to nutrition, posture, or living habits which might be causing the condition and which you yourself can correct without being told to do so by your doctor.

"A hale cobbler is better than a sick king," is an ancient maxim but its underlying truth still holds. Rare indeed is the individual who can surmount the obstacle of ill-health. Radiant, buoyant vitality provides the surest foundation for self-unfoldment and personality development. Almost any individual can capture or hold good health if he is willing to follow certain relatively simple rules of healthful living. True enough, some individuals are vested by heredity with greater physique or higher vitality than their fellows, which means that those not so vested may have to work a little harder and stick a little closer to the rules to get their results. Such closer adherence may be doubly beneficial. One physician has said that, "The augury for a long life is to have an individual sickly in his youth." In other words, those who learn early to take care of themselves, take care of themselves.

LENGTH OF LIFE INCREASING

The average length of life in the United States is today more than 70 years. In 1790 it was about 35 years. This remarkable increase has been achieved through medical research, medical attention, and a wider dissemination of knowledge as to personal hygiene and emotional balance. This chapter and the next three will attempt to boil down into plain statements those simple rules of physical living which have proved of use in lengthening life and, more importantly, in maintaining physical energy at a high level throughout life.

HOW TO LIVE A LONG TIME

So you'd like to live a long and useful life, would you? It's largely a matter of heredity, temperament, and wise living habits.

Many studies have been made of individuals who live to be 90 or longer. Eight factors are generally present:

1. *Good health.* They are rarely sick. They sleep well, reveal physical stamina, and avoid most chronic diseases.
2. *Physically active.* Throughout their lives, they keep their muscles alive, get exercise of one kind or another.
3. *They enjoy work.* Some have second and third careers. They don't retire to rocking chairs.
4. *Emotional maturity.* Optimism, poise under pressure, adjustment to change.
5. *Self-discipline.* In living habits, nutrition, alcohol, tobacco and coffee.
6. *Happy marriage.*
7. *Rural life.* Rural dwellers tend to outlive those who live in cities.
8. *Wise choice of forebears.* Four out of five who make it to 90 have parents, grandparents, or other close relatives who do the same. However, not all those with the same heredity make it; some through careful living live long beyond the years achieved by their forebears.

Here's a simple calculation you can make as to your own chances for a long life, based on parents and grandparents: Record the ages at death of those who have passed on. For those still living consult actuarial tables for life expectancy. Eliminate those who died accidental deaths. Calculate the average of the remainder. This is *your* expectancy. You can lessen it by excesses. You can increase it by the methods detailed in this book, for age is a number, not a physical condition. Industry's practice of retiring capable and healthy men and women at age 65 is a reprehensible waste of talent, a loss of productive energy, and a contributor to ego destruction.

If you live to what is euphemistically called "a ripe old age," however, you will have to accept that time erodes your youthful powers like the gusty autumn wind steals fiery leaves from the sturdy oak.

YOUR HEALTH–WORK AT IT

Whatever your physical deficiencies are, get after them. If you have fallen arches, get the advice of a foot specialist and follow it.

If you have athlete's foot or other skin diseases, you must clear them up. Pay attention to the hair and scalp; well-kept hair is a personality asset. Nose and throat conditions, or sinus difficulties, require that you have them treated. Sinus trouble, normally blamed on climatic conditions, often results from fatigue, loss of sleep, smoking, or the frequent use of cathartics. Take good care of your eyes—you'll never get another pair.

Our insurance friends tell us that mortality is higher among those who are underweight up to the age of 40, but among those who are overweight after the age of 40. Overweight in those under 40 has a tendency to slow up physical activity, but is not particularly dangerous until the middle life period has been passed, when overweight puts a tax upon the heart. As a general rule, a leeway of 10 percent above or below the average weight is considered a safe range.

An excellent way to keep yourself in fine fettle is to join a "health club." The facilities usually offered include a gymnasium, steam room, shower, massage, and sun lamp. Particularly if you lead a sedentary life, you should look into this possibility. The next time you are feeling sluggish, get one of these treatments. First, exercise commensurate with your present physical condition, then take a hot shower and thorough soaping; scrub the skin with a stiff brush; finish with a cool shower. Into the steam room with you. If you are underweight, stay only until perspiration breaks out all over your body; if you are overweight, stay a few minutes longer. Next a quick shower, tapering from warm to cold. Then a sun-lamp exposure, as directed by the attendant. After this, a massage, followed by an alcohol rub. Roll up in a sheet and sleep for at least half an hour. Try it—I guarantee that your body will be glowing, your heart exultant, your cares diminished.

ATTACK EACH MINOR AILMENT

Major ailments start as minor ailments. Bleeding gums, unattended, lead to dentures. A persistent cough, unheeded, may be the forerunner of lung trouble. A recurrent shoulder pain may end up as bursitis.

And so it goes. Don't ignore any repeated or enduring pain or upset, lest it erupt into something more serious. This warning does not mean to run to your medicine chest for every ache and pain.

But if an ache or pain continues or reappears, attack it with all the intelligence at your command—including a visit to your physician.

Forces in your body continually seek equilibrium, so that most conditions are healed by nature. But when it becomes apparent that Dame Nature can't do the job unassisted, that's the time for you to step in with diet, rest, mild medication, exercise, heat, and a positive frame of mind. If these fail, seek expert medical diagnosis and treatment.

SO YOU'RE OVERWEIGHT!

The tendency to obesity runs in families. Fat children will likely become fat adults and have fat children in turn. Fat children face emotional and physical difficulties. If you are fat, you should avoid sweets, "junk" food, between-meal snacks—and should get plenty of exercise.

But you say, I'm an adult. Is it too late to do something about my overweight?

Basic to weight reduction is a reduction in food intake (and hence calories), particularly carbohydrates—bread, potatoes, pasta, cornstarch, sugar, candy, and alcohol. Accompanying the reduction of carbohydrates should be a substitution of proteins—lean meats, poultry, fish, nuts, some cheeses. (We shall consider girth control in greater detail in Chapter 5.)

LAUGHTER—GOOD EXERCISE

Probably you never thought of hearty laughter as good exercise, but it is. It causes the diaphragm to massage the heart, thus making it beat faster. As a consequence, blood circulation increases, resulting in stimulation to abdominal organs such as stomach, liver, pancreas, spleen and gall bladder.

A good belly laugh also expands the lungs so that they take in more oxygen. That too, is good for you. So don't hesitate to seek out funny situations, or to laugh heartily when situations suggest it.

ARE YOU A "TYPE A" PERSON?

Medical researchers have pretty well proven that "Type A" persons are more likely to have heart attacks than "Type B" persons.

Type As are go-getters—overly aggressive, competitive, ambitious and constantly under time pressures. They talk, walk, and eat in a hurry, as though time were a scarce commodity, not to be wasted.

Type Bs are low pressure, more relaxed, patient, and deliberate. They work against a calendar rather than a clock, and believe there's always tomorrow.

If Type A persons have inadequate physical activity, eat improperly, are overweight and smoke excessively, they are almost surefire candidates for some form of coronary or organic disease. You can be ambitious and persevering without becoming a Type A personality. The American Heart Association tells how you can perform a death-defying act: "Have your blood pressure checked."

LOOK—TO YOUR EYES

If your eyes become diseased or injured, go to a competent eye specialist—fast. In any event, get a regular eye examination every two years. As you grow older, visual defects creep in which however are mostly correctible—near-sightedness, far-sightedness, astigmatism, vertical or lateral imbalance, depth perception. Uncorrected, these conditions can lead to accidents, headaches, upset stomachs and eyestrain.

Eyestrain can result from too much light, too little light, and reflected light (glare). Hence, you should consider what kind of illumination and how much, you are getting. Here are three rules to observe:

1. Avoid situations where your eyes are alternately subjected to much light and little light, especially if the alternation occurs several times per minute. If your desk faces a window, you may be enduring this condition. I'm sure you have observed how annoying this alternation can be, while driving beside a long row of trees with the sun shining between them.

2. Avoid strong light, or strongly reflected light, in your direct field of vision. Looking at a nearby light bulb, or a row of exposed lights, is harmful.

3. Try to arrange your lighting so that it is evenly distributed. Five 60-watt bulbs will normally be superior to one 300-watt bulb. Indirect lighting is usually superior to direct lighting, but greatly increases the needed wattage and hence the cost. Fluorescent lighting is usually excellent, and less expensive to operate.

If your eyes pain when first exposed to strong sunlight, wear sunglasses. However, if you normally wear glasses, you should have the same correction in your darkened glasses.

THE SENTRIES OF HEALTH

Standing at the portals of digestion are your teeth. When they are healthy they play an important role in the digestive process; when they're unhealthy they may play a negative role in mastication and may become a source of infection. Since they are important, they deserve your attention. The money you give to a dentist for regular attention is money well spent.

Teeth cavities result from sugar which is broken down into acids that attack calcium—a process that Vitamin D helps arrest. Reduction of sugar intake and prompt brushing—or use of a water pik—*after each meal* will slow up tooth decay.

Pyorrhea involves infection of the gums, bleeding, loosening of the teeth, and their eventual loss. Sometimes there is decalcification of jawbones, resulting in poor fitting dentures.

Candy, chewing gum, and sweet drinks are frequent causes of gum irritation and tooth decay—especially if your diet is deficient in protein and calcium. Don't ignore your teeth—they'll get revenge if you do.

NOISE

You may pay a heavy toll in efficiency for the noises to which you are subjected throughout the day. The fact that you may not be conscious of most of them in no way alters this fact. Your body has to adjust to repetitive or unexpected sounds, honking horns, blaring radios, noisy TVs, screeches, high-intensity whistles, or threatening rumbles. Some of these sounds cause subconscious fear responses—heart action, digestion, blood pressure, muscular contractions.

If you are subjected to noise at work, at home, or while sleeping, here are some things you can do: (1) prevent or lessen noise at its source; (2) get away from it; (3) shut it out; (4) blot up sound waves before they reach your ears.

Don't hesitate to wage a campaign against loud radios, blaring

TVs, motorists who lean on their horns, pre-dawn garbage collection banging, barking dogs, and so forth. The federal government has finally classed noise as a form of environmental pollution, and has passed a law (OSHA) for noise protection of people at work. Make your own laws for home protection. There are available accoustical materials to mop up sound waves, and other materials to cushion vibrations which create sound waves.

Long-continued noises—and especially loud noises—can cause deafness. Advancing age results in an inability to hear higher frequencies or to separate speech from background sounds; individuals suffering these defects are "hard of hearing" but can generally be helped by modern hearing aids.

Don't delude yourself by saying, "Sound doesn't bother me." It does—whether you know it or not. In fact, psychologists believe that city din, office clatter, and workshop roar contribute to making a driving, restless, nervous personality (Type A).

ARTHRITIS, ANYONE?

Yes, almost every one over the age of 30, whether they know it or not, suffers from it.

For the most part, arthritis is incurable, but it can be alleviated, under the supervision of a competent physician. The first step is a proper diagnosis. The physician has quite an array of treatments at his command: aspirin, cortisone, ACTH, rest, diet, weight reduction, massage, exercise, dry heat, hot baths, hypodermic injections, emotional equanimity, X-rays, and other aids.

Above all avoid quack cures, copper bracelets, rabbit's feet, weird foods, overdosing with vitamins or minerals, mystery drugs, and other "miracles." You'll learn to live with your arthritis.

CANCER—NO. 1 KILLER

In taking care of your health, you should become aware of America's three worst killers: cancer, cardiovascular (heart) diseases, and diabetes. There are many things you can do to avoid these dread diseases, or to live with them if you are ensnared. The object of singling out these three diseases is to increase your awareness of them so that you will get complete physical examinations annually, follow your doctor's orders faithfully, read to increase your knowledge of your body and follow healthful living habits.

Can you do anything to prevent cancer? Accumulating evidence suggests that you can. Mormons and Seventh Day Adventists (who refrain from alcohol, and tobacco, and stress healthy emotional attitudes) die of cancer at half the rate of other people. Investigators believe that such a life-style, combined with peace of mind, a well-balanced diet of simple, unprocessed foods, and avoidance of overweight hold back would-be cancer cells.

There are rare but authenticated cases on record of sufferers from active cancers who have licked the condition by meditation and positive thinking. It is theorized that their strong belief has activated the body's defense mechanisms.

Most ailments get better by themselves. Medicines may set up favorable chemical conditions for healing to take place, but the restoration of balance is done by your body. Sometimes the best medicine is an optimistic frame of mind—coupled with regular check-ups.

WANT TO AVOID THE NO. 2 KILLER?

The most common cause of heart attack is fatty deposits (cholesterol) in arteries leading to the heart, narrowing the passage (occlusion), a condition known as "atherosclerosis." Usually, the condition can be spotted by an electrocardiogram (EKG) which charts the regularity or irregularity of the heartbeat.

Research indicates that blood cholesterol levels can be elevated by emotional stress. For example, a study of public accountants showed these levels higher just before April 15th, the income tax deadline, than several months later. Other research has shown that a regimen of diet, exercise, and drugs can reverse the accumulation of cholesterol, but that the reversal may take several years.

Sometimes, heart attacks cause severe chest pains, sometimes the pains are mild, and hence passed off as mere digestive disturbances or extreme fatigue.

Four ways to avoid heart attacks are: (1) do not smoke; (2) avoid overweight; (3) do sensible exercises; (4) avoid negative emotional stress.

Most adults have some degree of atherosclerosis; many have had unrecognized heart attacks which however will likely show up in an EKG (also known as ECG). Repeated EKG recordings over some years will reveal whether dangerous conditions are developing. You will be wise to get a thorough annual physical examination, which will include the EKG.

If you, and other members of your family have a history of long-standing high blood pressure, you are a likely candidate for a heart attack. So look to the diet and moderate exercise program *before* you have an attack.

DIABETES–KILLER NO. 3

More people die annually from diabetes and related diseases than are killed in accidents.

You don't have to wait until you suffer an insatiable thirst before you suspect incipient diabetes. An annual or semiannual urinalysis and blood test will help you catch it in its early stages when it is most readily controlled. There are simple tests which can even spot potential diabetes.

Doctors estimate that five million Americans already know that they have diabetes—but that another five million have it but don't know it.

Diabetes is an inherited condition whereby your pancreas does not generate enough insulin to convert your intake of starches and sugars. Since it is inherited, you can't prevent it, but you can learn to live with it by means of a prescribed diet, insulin, exercise, and maintenance of a normal weight. Constant daily care is necessary.

ARE YOU A SLAVE TO THE WEATHER?

Ever stop to wonder why some days you feel peppy, others, mopey? Or, one day everything goes wrong, the next day you find smooth sailing? Maybe you should blame the barometer or thermometer.

Convincing world-wide research has shown that when barometric pressure is low and falling: (1) your tissues hold more water and, consequently, swell; (2) arthritic tendencies become more noticeable; (3) some folks (most?) tend to be nervous and irritable; (4) crimes of violence rise.

Temperature, too, affects human behavior. For example:

1. Cool weather is invigorating; hot, enervating. However, extremes in either direction can place unwanted adaptation on your body. You have long since learned that if the air you are breathing is extremely hot, humid, or cold, your mental initiative and physical energy will both be sluggish.

2. July and August are the worst offenders. Mental effectiveness then is down, crime up.

3. However, weather change is stimulating; monotonous weather (good or bad) can be depressing. Air-conditioned atmosphere can help if you don't alternate between it and hot muggy conditions. A temperature of 64 degrees seems to be most beneficial, both day and night.

Instead of being a slave to the weather, learn to make it your ally. When a storm is on the way, indicated by a falling barometer, that's the time to do routine or physical work. When it rains cats and dogs, that's beastly weather; the only thing it's good for is to reduce the price of vegetables. When rain or snow is falling outside, take on nontaxing mental jobs.

When the storms have passed, and a high pressure area is on the way, tackle difficult problems or study new subjects.

Be your own meteorologist—be weather smart.

GET AN ANNUAL CHECKUP

It's amazing how many people fail to get an annual physical examination. "I feel fine," they say, "why bother?" Subconsciously, they may be afraid of what it might turn up. Yet most ailments *caught early,* can be cured, or at worst, slowed up.

Modern medical science has developed a large arsenal of sophisticated weapons—physical, chemical, electrical and electronic —for diagnosis and treatment.

Conventional X-rays are normally useful in diagnosing conditions involving hard substances such as bones, calcium deposits, gallstones, and so forth. The body scanner is useful with soft tissues such as tumors, blood clots, enlargement of internal organs, and spinal cord abnormalities. In conjunction with miniature computers, body scanners pass an X-ray beam through the body, scanning a horizontal cross section, one level at a time.

As another example of modern practice, consider various uses of electrical current: speeding up bone and other healing, straightening an abnormally curved spine, relieving chronic pain, healing skin ulcers and bed sores, relieving abdominal pain following surgery, easing drug-resistant epilepsy, stimulating muscles, and so forth.

When things go awry physically, it is the mark of intelligence to find the cause, and to help your body correct the condition with all the facilities that medical science can supply.

ALLERGIES

An allergy is a hypersensitive reaction to specific foreign substances which are breathed, touched, tasted, or swallowed. It is usually manifested by sneezing, skin rashes, itching and watery eyes—sometimes by asthmatic attacks or indigestion.

Asthma can lead to spasms of coughing, bronchitis, and emphysema (over-inflated lungs with destruction of lung tissue). The last named can be helped by exercises which improve use of the diaphragm in exhaling.

Skin rashes and itching hives can be caused by certain foods (strawberries and sea foods are common offenders), or by direct contact (sea nettles, or poison ivy, for example).

Scratch tests can usually determine the irritants which are causing trouble. However, infections, emotional problems, lack of rest, and exercise can aggravate allergic tendencies. The easiest treatment is to avoid the irritants. Antihistamine drugs ease the sneezing, itching, and runny nose, but may make you feel "dopey." A course of injections can usually build up considerable immunity.

If you suffer from some form of allergy, you will likely battle it most of your life, though advancing years often bring some degree of immunization. Allergies are annoying, sometimes crippling. If you are a sufferer, learn to control yours early in life.

SELF-APPRAISAL

Figure 6 gives you an opportunity to appraise ten factors which bear upon your general health. Some of these factors have been discussed in this chapter; others will be considered in chapters which follow.

FIGURE 6
An honest look at my health

In each of the ten lines below, check the block which comes closest to your self-appraisal. If you can't decide between two blocks, check the narrow space between them. Be honest, but not harsh with yourself!

Factor	2	3	4	5	6	7	8	9	10
Weight-height ratio	Overweight— I'm fat!		Heavy build		Average for my age		I'm slender		Lean, but not emaciated
Digestion	Chronic stomach or intestinal upsets		More than 6 upsets over last 12 months		Three to six upsets		Have had one or two		No upsets over last 12 months
Elimination	Chronic diarrhea		Take laxative several times each month		Occasional constipation		Rarely have bowel problems		Adequate movement daily
Eyesight	Very bad— cannot be corrected		Repeated eyesight trouble		Have an uncorrectible problem in one eye		20/20 vision with glasses		20/20 vision without glasses
Alcohol	I drink more than 25 oz. of hard liquor weekly		15 to 25 oz. of hard liquor per week		14 oz. or less per week		I drink beer or wine only		I don't drink at all
Drugs	I'm hooked on one or more kinds		I take too many pain killers		I take too many sleeping pills		Occasional sleeping, pain or other drug		I take no drugs
Tobacco	I smoke about two packs per day		One pack per day		Possibly one pack per week		I haven't smoked for one to five years		I haven't smoked for five years or more
Exercise	Less than one hour per week walking		Less than two hours per week walking		Possibly three hours per week walking		Engage in active physical sports		Daily setting-up exercises
Impairments	I have a serious, permanent impairment		Handicaps limit my job effectiveness		I am battling several minor handicaps		Occasionally I suffer from one handicap		I have no physical impairments
Hobbies	None		I'm too busy to indulge		I follow a hobby occasionally		I dabble at one or two hobbies		I get great satisfaction from one or more

3

Keep your muscles alive

An old saying runs: Keep your muscles alive, and they'll keep you alive. Physiological research supports this truism.

Much of your body is muscle tissue, of two kinds: voluntary, such as in your arms or legs, and involuntary, such as those muscles involved in digestion, breathing, blood circulation, or the heart itself. At one time it was believed that you had no conscious control over involuntary muscles, but recent studies in biofeedback suggest that you can learn to influence these muscles to some extent.

Muscles exert their power by contracting; they pull, but do not push. By relaxing, they reverse the pulling process. Normally there are opposing (antagonist) muscles which pull in the opposite direction, thus offering a counter force. The muscles you use to pull up a sticking window may be different from those needed to close it.

EXERCISE

The physical body is a machine, and as such it is intended to be operated. Disuse of muscles causes them to lose their power and may even cause loss of their effectiveness. With muscular activity the circulation rate of the blood increases from two to eight times, with many resulting benefits. Similarly, the perspiration rate increases, along with the increased functioning of lungs and other organs of the body. These changes mean deep breathing, removal of waste products, stimulation of sluggish areas of the body, acceleration of organs and a number of other benefits. Not to mention the increased power of the muscles being exercised.

Competitive sports and games are good for young people, but may be too taxing for those in middle or later life. Heart and lung development are important in early life, as well as the character development that comes from learning to lose in competition. There is an interest element in games and competitive sports which is not inherent in mere exercise. The acquisition of skill in sports is in itself a joy. However, those who have passed the point where they can safely indulge in the more violent forms of exercise will still do well to build up health habits which include regular muscular exercise. Golf, brisk walking, swimming, calisthenics, and bowling are forms of exercise which can be undertaken by almost any one at most any time of life. Yet a Gallup poll revealed that 43 percent of American adults do no deliberate walking outside their regular work and 58 percent take no systematic exercise.

Consistent use is good for a muscle, for it keeps open the channels that feed blood to it. Persons who exercise regularly require less oxygen to perform a given amount of work than those who do not exercise regularly. Hearts of athletes, for example, pump more blood with fewer beats per minute than those of nonathletes. Consistent exercise also increases both the capacity and efficiency of lungs. And so-called body-tone is largely muscle-tone. In today's muscles, tomorrow's muscle power already is stirring.

A railroad track worker repeatedly lifts a 30-pound tamp 6 inches, and drops it on loose earth to pack it tight. A coal heaver shovels coal into a blazing furnace, facing enervating heat with each shovelful. Three furniture movers inch a large piano up a flight of stairs. And all these men grow stronger in the doing, acquire increased capacity to do more of the same type of work.

SO YOU HAVE A DESK JOB

In advanced nations, progress up the economic ladder frequently means being chained to a desk, or other sedentary, job. This kind of task usually means more mental work and less physical activity. In turn, the rate of blood circulation decreases, particularly in the lower legs, risking varicose veins and clotting (thrombosis). Sometimes a part of a clot breaks off and travels to heart or lungs (embolism).

If you have a desk job, get up and walk around occasionally. This action, like all forms of exercise, increases circulation in the veins, fights flabby muscles, increases breathing, improves functioning of the diaphragm, aids digestion, and stimulates bowel action.

Persons who fail to exercise regularly fall prey to a whole host of ailments and diseases which otherwise would never attack them.

> A 46-year-old lady, following a serious operation, gave up on life. She just sat all the time. She put on weight. Both legs began to swell and she became short of breath with slight exertion. All these signs, she thought, confirmed her self-diagnosis that the end was near. Her family physician could find no dangerous vital signs, and talked her into a long walk each day. Within a few weeks, all negative signs had disappeared. She ultimately passed away at 86.

Doctors say that the habit of walking—preferably brisk walking—each day will do more for an unhappy but reasonably healthy person than all the prescriptions they can write.

HOW ABOUT JOGGING?

Depending on your general physical condition, jogging may be good, or bad, for you. If you are overweight, in poor health, or beyond middle life, don't jog unless so advised by your physician.

> One of my friends, the late psychologist Henry Link, told of a counselee who was so discouraged with his life that he wanted to end it. Link suggested that he go in for jogging, which might bring on a heart attack and so achieve his aim. In a few weeks the man returned, saying that he felt so much better, he had changed his mind about suicide.

As a safe rule, jogging is for Americans in their 20s or early 30s—and then only after a thorough physical examination. For the rest of us, a long brisk walk through the woods, with curious eyes for nature all around, will prove better than a grimly imposed jog.

EFFICIENT USE OF MUSCLES

A great deal of your initiative results in physical energy: you do something. Your muscles are put to work to protect or to advance you in some way.

There is some most efficient work rate for each muscle you use. If your work or daily life requires you to use certain muscles repeatedly, it will pay you to experiment until you discover the best pace for each repetitive activity.

> The summer before I entered college, I worked in a Pennsylvania coal mine. The first hour or so I swung a pick with huge sweeps, as though I were trying to loosen all the coal in a few blows. Soon, to my relief, an old miner showed me how to dig with short blows, each of which loosened a small quantity but which in the long run produced more coal than my heroic method. More important to me was the fact that the new way didn't tire my arms and shoulders. My working pace was right for the particular set of muscles being used.

SOME EXERCISE FALLACIES

There are many false notions associated with exercising, especially in the case of athletics and other strenuous activity. Here are some of them:

1. Get candy or sugar before heavy exercise. Wrong. It may be O.K. *after* a mile race, or three sets of tennis.
2. Salt tablets will prevent fatigue. Wrong. Your normal diet supplies enough salt, unless you sweat like a race horse.
3. Eat a beefsteak before strenuous athletics. Wrong, and a probable waste of your money. Violent exercise too soon after any meal may cause you to "pop your cookies." Super-foods don't transmute into super-performance.
4. Don't drink water while exercising. Wrong. Dehydration puts a strain on your muscles, heart included.
5. After heavy exercise, immediately put on a sweater. Wrong. Give your body a chance to cool down to normal, then put on the sweater to avoid chilliness.
6. Follow a hot shower with a cold one. Wrong. Your heart may not be able to stand the resulting constriction of blood vessels.
7. Huge muscles mean great strength. Maybe yes, maybe no.

Muscle fibers can be strengthened without enlarging; or can get fatter with little increase in power.

8. Strenuous exercise is better for you than mild exercise. A dubious belief. Much depends on your age, physical condition and objective. Your aim should be general health rather than Herculean strength, unless you're going to compete for the world weight-lifting championship.

Every now and then, some promoter advertises some exercise gimmick which will do wonders for you—if you enroll for his course or buy his equipment. If you have the will power to exercise regularly and sensibly, you don't need to pay out money to do what nature intended you to do in the first place.

TWO KINDS OF FATIGUE

A feeling of fatigue can result from two causes: (1) continued use of muscles; (2) negative emotions. Fatigue is one of nature's protective devices to warn you against dangerous stresses and strains—physical, mental, or emotional. Thus if you're sick, you probably feel tired, too. Nature is then discouraging energy-consuming activity to mobilize your energies for resisting the disease or stress that is making you sick. Likewise, continuous use of a muscle can tire it.

If you sit at a desk all week, and then indulge in some heavy exercise for a few hours over the weekend, you may destroy up to 30 percent of your red blood corpuscles. So you may reduce the reserve supply of oxygen available to be "borrowed" for mental or physical activity and reduce the number of carriers (corpuscles) on hand to transport oxygen to the muscles and brain. So don't be a weekend athlete.

Dieting too strenuously can abet fatigue by reducing the calorie intake. Muscles need fat and protein as well as carbohydrates (starches and sugars). Fatigue effects can be postponed, but not dissipated, by the caffeine in coffee, tea and cola drinks. Alcohol and tobacco in small amounts have somewhat the same effect; in large amounts they do more harm than good. Pills and drugs are dangerous devices, except under skilled medical supervision.

The feeling of fatigue from negative emotions is sometimes known as "false fatigue." Here we are dealing with something quite different from genuine fatigue. Lack of interest, boredom, or a feeling of monotony usually precedes this type of fatigue feeling. Its results, in lowered productivity, can be quite as severe as the effects of genuine fatigue. We shall deal with it in later chapters.

COMMAND MUSCLES TO RELAX

Emotions can keep muscles tensed; they can use up reserve chemicals in the muscles and so stop the regeneration of energy. Then no amount of directly applied will power can get more than a few additional flickers from the enfeebled fibers.

You may reveal outward signs of this struggle by swinging a foot while seated, clearing your throat frequently, biting or picking at your fingernails, clenching your jaws, fidgeting with your clothes, toying with coins or other small objects, doodling, pencil chewing, or knuckle-cracking. Many of these are devices you have found successful in relieving tension. At the same time they are evidences of that tension.

You can relax muscles by conscious thought. Prove it—right now. The chances are that some of your muscles are tensed—in the neck, jaw, face, shoulders, abdomen, limbs. Let them down a notch. Another notch, maybe, until they feel limp.

To continue this experiment, suddenly tighten as many muscles of your body as you can. Hold this condition and note how uncomfortable you feel. If you were able to hold such muscle rigidity, it would rapidly deplete so many chemical elements of your body that you would faint, or tremble, or have to lie down.

Now relax them all . . . more . . . some more. What body peace! All during your waking hours:

1. The brain and other parts of the nervous system send instructions to organs and muscles of the body.
2. Organs and muscles return information to the central nervous system. If they report trouble, the central system gears the body to overcome it—including instructions to muscles to get ready for action (i.e., by tenseness).

If the reporting stations indicate that all is well, however, no tensing instructions are issued to the muscles. This means that if you succeed in relaxing muscles by conscious thought, they will send "all is well" messages to the brain; the muscles will stay relaxed (as long as you avoid negative emotions, which would elicit more tensing instructions.) And if the muscles stay relaxed, they recover their chemical powers for action: they are no longer fatigued.

So when you are under stress, particularly emotional stress, consciously relax your muscles. Idle your motor even though you feel like stripping your gears. When you can't sleep, relax your muscles. When you feel off center, have no appetite, no energy, no desire—relax your muscles, one at a time. Get yourself as limp as a child's rag doll. And stay that way until energy resurges within you.

You may have to practice a while before you learn to control the relaxation of your muscles. But it is so important that some psychiatrists have regular exercises that they teach to their patients, including concentration and self-discipline. (In this connection, a later chapter will discuss transcendental meditation.)

IF YOU'RE A TYPE A PERSON

In the previous chapter, we mentioned the Type A personality— the aggressive, competitive, clock-fighter—who is prone to stomach ulcers and heart attacks. When these individuals end up in hospitals, they are directed to exercise regularly and admonished to relax.

If you're a tense Type A, try these three approaches for the relaxation part:

1. Tighten muscles *hard,* one at a time, saying to yourself, "My leg (arm, neck, hand, shoulder, etc.) muscle," as you tense it. Then relax. Relax more. In this way you get the feel of each identified muscle when tensed and when completely relaxed.
2. List various things in your home and work life which cause you to tense up. Recall some of the worst; maybe just the memory will cause muscles to contract. Think relaxation of those muscles; the intensity of the memory will lessen or fade.
3. Rearrange your daily life to eliminate or at least mitigate the offending circumstances. Even when they reappear, spot the particular muscles which have tensed, and relax them utterly. With practice you'll win this battle.

GAIN AN EXTRA HOUR EVERY DAY

Proper sleep habits can contribute to your well-being by restoring muscle energy and by allowing you more time for leisure or self-improvement activities.

Most of the recuperative powers of sleep occur in the first two hours. You get about as much benefit from those two hours as from the remaining six. The last hour of an eight-hour stretch contributes about 4 percent of the total recuperation that has occurred. If you can avoid the necessity for that 4 percent, you automatically have found a way to contribute one hour of time to your productive day.

Take a cat nap after each meal, and particularly after the noon meal, and you may get the same benefit as an hour and a half of sleep. Such cat naps should not total more than half an hour throughout the day; it is not even necessary to get fully to sleep as long as you lie flat, and relax completely. After each cat nap you should become muscularly active gradually, to stir up the circulation again and to help digest the food in the stomach.

If you have been excited, either happily or unhappily, the hangover from these emotional processes may prevent you from sleeping. Thus it is that old folks, as a general rule, find it simple to get to sleep because their lives are uneventful. Part of your problem is to put monotony into the picture at the time you want to go to sleep. The classic method of counting sheep is an example.

SOME SLEEP HINTS

Sleep in a quiet room. If there are sounds present, these should be monotonous, such as the ticking of a clock. Sudden noises should be kept out. You are trying to achieve a state of muscular relaxation (aided by monotonous conditions) that is conducive to sleep. If you live in a neighborhood where trains, taxis, or buses bring loud or shrill noises into your bedroom, you will do well to move to another neighborhood. The adjustments that the body makes to these sounds while you are sleeping may not be realized by you but they are present nevertheless, and they use up precious energy.

You should sleep on a bed that is fairly hard, and one that is wide enough for you to do some tossing about. Authorities feel that this width should be a minimum of 39 inches. Sleep alone so that you will not be disturbed. A cramped position can prevent proper relaxation. Prevent outside lights or sunrise from shining in your eyes. Avoid a lumpy mattress or too soft a mattress. Use large sheets and blankets; also blankets that are warm but light in weight.

A room that is too cold can consume blood sugar energy. A room that is too warm can force rapid breathing and heartbeat.

A tepid or warm tub bath before retiring is likely to facilitate sleep; a shower may be more stimulating than relaxing. Build up regular hours for sleep and stay pretty close to those hours. If you know you are going to be out late, try to get a half hour or an hour's sleep before going out.

Above all, avoid dependence on drugs to help you sleep; once you build this habit, you will find it difficult to break away from it. Their accumulated effect will lower your energy throughout the following day. Moreover, medical researchers aver that many of the much-advertised sleep aids are nothing more than placebos—you imagine that they are effective and hence do actually sleep. Research suggests that some sleep-aid drugs are actually harmful.

If you follow the practice advocated in this book of keeping alive all your muscles through activity, you will dispose of waste products through the circulatory and eliminative processes of the body. This condition in itself is conducive to repose. However, if some time you are greatly fatigued because of strenuous muscular activity, you may have to aid the removal of waste products by means of a very hot bath, a steam bath, sweating, and massage.

Sleep is one of the important building blocks of vital living. For many individuals it is merely nature's way of correcting excesses and negligence: for a few individuals, sleep is harnessed to the development of high vitality.

PLAY—FOR YOUR HEALTH

We all know what happens to Jack when he does all work and no play. This maxim, in one form or another, appears in both ancient and modern literature of most nations: it is a truism about human beings.

But lack of play may make Jack more than a dull boy—it may make him a sick man.

Play is elemental, primitive. It releases positive emotions. Play doesn't have to be a sports activity. It can be "visiting" with a neighbor, listening to the kind of music you enjoy, reading a novel, watching the birds in a nearby woods, playing cards, or collecting stamps.

The ability to have fun, to find joyousness in little things, makes the eyes bright, the cheeks flushed, the voice animated, the head high. In short, it makes for health and happiness.

So learn anew to play—please!

YOUR POSTURE

Good posture pays, bad posture betrays.

By building good posture habits, you impress others that you are a winner, not bowed down with life's burdens or old age slump. By standing tall you may avoid a pain in the neck. By avoiding rounded shoulders, whether sitting or standing, you may prevent back pains. You will breathe deeper, avoid crowding your heart and consequently send more oxygen to your brain. You may take unwanted pressure off stomach and abdominal organs, find relief from chronic fatigue.

To test whether you have good posture, stand in your natural position before a full-length mirror. Your side view should show vertical alignment from earlobe through shoulder, hip bone, and ankle bone. Any deviation suggests swayback, duck feet (flat feet), or forward head.

When humans got off "all fours" and stood erect on two legs, they put quite a burden on their spines. Failure of supporting muscles to maintain the proper erect position causes abdominal organs to sag (pot belly); exaggerated rump (lordosis); exaggerated pushing back of shoulders (swayback); and low back pain. With pain comes further muscular spasm, causing greater difficulty of correction.

In the correct erect posture, you "stand tall" with chin and abdomen in, shoulders back. Try this position, standing with your back against a wall.

When doing heavy lifting, bend the legs and let them do most of the work, not your back muscles. When sitting at a desk or work bench, refrain from a leaning forward position that puts a pull on the "small of your back."

Here are some exercises to help you capture good posture. Do only a few at first, gradually adding more each week as your muscles grow stronger.

1. First learn the correct position of head, shoulders, abdomen, and hips outlined above. The full-length mirror will help.
2. Chin down, pull abdominal muscles in while standing.
3. Tighten buttock muscles to tilt the pelvis up in front. Hold. Count five. Relax.
4. On hard chair, sit up straight with both feet on the floor. Avoid soft, overstuffed furniture.
5. Sitting, clasp hands behind your back; sit erect; bring shoulder blades together while pulling downward with clasped hands. Hold. Count five. Relax.
6. Lie flat on your back, legs bent, knees high, feet on the floor. Tighten buttocks and abdominal muscles, chin in, pressing your neck and the small of your back hard against the floor. Hold. Count five. Relax.
7. Lying with back and neck flat, raise each leg bent, then straighten it high.
8. Brace your feet under a heavy chair and do sit-ups.
9. Lying on your tummy, clasp hands behind your back, raise your head, arching your back, and drawing buttocks together. Hold, count five, relax.

In four weeks, you should notice a change in posture, back pains and muscle tone. Try it. You'll like it.

SOME DON'T KNOW HOW TO WALK

Do you duck waddle, with your toes turned way out? If so, you'll likely get flat feet, or muscle problems in ankles, knees, hip joints, or lower back. Per contra, if you're pigeontoed, you place different kinds of stress on ankles and knee joints.

You can avoid both these distortions by consciously taking a longer stride, feet straight forward. Walk erect, shoulders back, and as the Army sergeant inelegantly puts it, "Suck in your gut!"

Walking is good exercise; walking tall is excellent exercise; walking briskly is therapeutic; walking a lot is physical wisdom.

Subconsciously, others judge you by your posture and walk. So stand erect and walk with unchained feet.

4
Want more pep?

Some folks seem to have boundless energy, a happy resultant of many factors working together. Previous chapters have discussed basic health and the importance of regular muscular activity.

This chapter will consider contributors to and detractors from, energy. The chapter which follows will review the importance of diet as it affects both health and energy.

ENERGY ADDS ZEST TO LIFE

You rotate the tires on your car to prevent one from wearing out faster than the others. Follow a similar practice in your life. If you have been in a routine grind for some time, do something totally different—a trip, some new sport, some unusual amusement. If a gay uninhibited life begins to pall on you, try solitude and meditation. If you have become self-centered, call up some friends, write letters, do deeds of kindness. Tired of housework? Listen to some records. Stale from studying? Go work in your garden. Weary of gardening? Do some studying.

By rotating your activities, you can prevent any one of them from depressing your morale, which in turn causes some organ to bear the brunt of the emotional pressure created.

Scientists have attempted to measure the effects of environment. In one study, a man was paid to do nothing 24 hours per day. He was fed; wore goggles that admitted foggy light; his ears, hands, and arms were covered. Tests showed that he lost some of his problem-solving ability; he could not concentrate, was bored, lost his initiative, had disturbed muscle control, suffered hallucinations. The experimenter concluded that human beings may be psychologically at the mercy of their environment to a much greater degree than they think.

Briefly, then, scientists conclude that environment plays an important part in our attitudes and emotional states, and hence in our ability to produce copious energy. They feel it is just as important to marry the right life as the right mate. (We shall consider this topic in some detail in a later chapter.)

RECOGNITION AS A SOURCE OF ENERGY

Let us consider four principal sources of psychological energizing. The first is recognition which comes to you from others, and hence can only be influenced by you indirectly. Some of its forms are praise for something you have done; favorable mention in public, or in a publication; a diploma, certificate, title, medal, badge or other insignia of accomplishment; an increase in earnings; a promotion; election to a coveted office; acceptance as a leader; friendship, displayed and spoken; affection from family members and friends; acceptance into some group that you consider worthwhile. All these forms of recognition are important energizers, because they yield happy states of mind that release energy. To enjoy them, however, you must give before you can hope to get. Recognition from others must be earned; it cannot be demanded. You do things for others, qualify yourself for higher responsibilities, work for the aims of an organization, give friendship and affection, take the point of view of a group you would join. If you do these things freely and consistently, without thought that you are buying popularity, energizing recognition will come to you.

NEW INTEREST CAN RELEASE ENERGY

The second psychological source of surging energy is interest. Most of us get into narrow ruts; we do the same things, in the same places, with the same people, over and over again. These activities become humdrum, monotonous, boring. As a consequence, we think we are "tired."

> Some friends of mine, a middle-aged married couple, worked in their garden all day Saturday. By 9:00 p.m. they were dozing, trying to summon enough energy to get to bed.
>
> Then a group of friends descended upon them with a crazy idea: "We're driving to Atlantic City for a dip in the ocean. Won't you join us?"
>
> They did, laughing, singing, swimming in the moonlight, hot dogs at midnight, home at 2:00 a.m. Tired? Not a thought of it; instead they felt exhilarated, reinvigorated. And they woke up the next morning feeling refreshed both in body and spirit.

Undoubtedly, you have had some similar experiences, but you may not have caught their significance: Interest can release galvanizing energy.

> I know a chap who for years has made unusual New Year's resolutions. Each New Year's Eve he writes on 52 3 x 5-inch cards things he intends to do during the coming year. Here are some from his last year's batch:
>
> *Attend a service at the local Moslem church.*
> *Go bowling.*
> *Cut out a linoleum block to make my own Christmas cards.*
> *Write to some friend I haven't contacted for ten years.*
> *Attend a basketball game.*
> *Take some child to the circus.*
>
> Whenever he feels tired and dispirited, he shuffles his cards and selects one at random. If the season is wrong for it, he takes another. But he does what the card commands. Even if he's not tired or dispirited, he'll take on one of the activities in a spirit of adventure.
>
> This I don't have to tell you: he's a most interesting fellow, and one of the peppiest individuals I have ever known.
>
> This I do have to tell you: he's now 76 years young.

SATISFYING SPECIFIC WANTS STIMULATES ENERGY

The third exciter of energy is feeling the need to satisfy wants. These wants must be specific if they are to motivate you. For example, you may crave:

1. Wealth—so you can have and do the specific things you want.
2. Fame—for some particular knowledge or accomplishment.
3. Power over certain individuals to accomplish specific aims.
4. Adulation from certain individuals or groups.
5. Social prestige in relation to particular social groups.
6. Sensual satisfactions—sex, food, color, taste, rhythm, sounds.
7. Service to others—helping them, bringing them peace or other forms of happiness.
8. Creativeness—with words, ideas, mathematical relationships, or physical materials.
9. Participation—in specific movements, under strong leadership.
10. Spiritual identification with a Higher Power.

Strong motivation can overcome the debilitation which usually attends poor health. The fact that very few overcome this debility makes all the more remarkable the performance of those who do.

GROW UP EMOTIONALLY—YOU'LL HAVE MORE ENERGY

The fourth source of energy release is emotional maturity. Immature reactions to situations inhibit, prevent; mature reactions release, permit energy to flow. Patience, persistence, courage, weighing alternatives, decisiveness, tolerance, compassion, forgiveness—these and similar attributes mark the emotionally mature person.

Every day of your life you produce large quantities of energy—some to maintain your body at a 98° temperature, some to do mental and muscular work. A few individuals seem to possess almost unlimited reserves of such energy, and are as zealous as a dog on a flea hunt. Don't envy them; you, too, can feel you are bursting with vitality most of the time, simply by understanding how to use the four energy instigators given above, each of which will be explored in depth in later chapters.

EMERGENCIES CALL FORTH STORED ENERGY

Tonight you are awakened by an acrid smell of smoke. You investigate, but cannot locate the source. Back to bed, but not to sleep. The smell of smoke intensifies; this time you trace it to a pile of oily rags in your basement, left there by a careless painter. You pour a bucket of water on the rags and go back to bed. No sleep. You read for an hour, try once more to get off to sleep. But the odor of smoke is increasing again. You investigate and you find a second pile of oily rags. Now you search every corner, every box in your basement for more rags, soak them with water, toss them onto the driveway back of your house. As you do so, you notice the sun is about to rise: you have been awake all night, yet you are not tired.

Where did all that muscular energy come from? Although you know you couldn't repeat this performance every night, you nevertheless had a stockpile of energy somewhere. You drew heavily upon it. Sometime, in some way, you will have to replenish it. How should you best do this? Could you safely use some portion of reserve physical energy for a higher pace of living, provided you learned the knack of replacing your withdrawals? What would it do for your life if you continually utilized only 5 percent more physical energy than you now use?

These are important questions. If you answer them wisely, your whole life may become more satisfying, more productive.

NEGATIVE EMOTIONS CAN CAUSE FATIGUE

Negative emotions differ from positive emotions in one important respect: they are accompanied by tense muscles. Subconsciously the body is being readied for attack, defense, or retreat. *Any* long-enduring negative emotion can deplete your reserves, can make you feel fatigued. You can exhaust yourself with futile hate. You can squander your physical strength by wallowing in mental pools of apprehension. You can paralyze normal physical activity with sustained grief. You can devitalize your life with loneliness. You can undermine your energies with the burden of guilt. Yet, as we shall see in Chapter 13, all these parasites that prey upon your physical vitality can be lessened in intensity—or eliminated from your life entirely!

YOU CAN CHANGE YOUR ATTITUDES

If you have learned to operate a typewriter by the hunt, peck, and erase system, it is not easy to break your bad habits and acquire the touch system. But if you have learned bad thinking habits, it's relatively simple to break them: you simply substitute good ones, and the bad ones soon disappear. Your principal problem is to learn to recognize your own negative attitudes. When you can identify some state of mind as fear, hate, guilt, loneliness, grief, or other anxiety, you then can realize that it is producing negative emotion power, and is therefore harmful to health and peace of mind.

When you feel confident, cheerful, courageous, determined, forgiving, friendly, loving, understanding, tolerant, resigned, poised, calm and at peace with God and man—then you are creating positive emotion power. This condition is benign to your health and happiness. Take advantage of such surges of energy. These are times for accomplishment, for taking on new challenges. These periods are precious—don't waste them.

At first it may seem difficult for you to believe that the thought can create the fact, that positive states of mind can bring abundant health and a joyous life. You may think your problem is financial, for example. Yet you will surely admit that it is more important to make a life than a living. Moreover, you have long since discovered that miserable thoughts bring feelings of miserable health. Why should it not work in reverse: joyous thoughts bring joyous feelings, vibrant health and emotion power for accomplishment.

DETRACTORS OF ENERGY

Digestive disturbances can throw you off balance physically, with consequent loss of energy. If you repeatedly suffer from stomach or liver upsets, indigestion, diarrhea, or constipation, you need to seek out and eliminate the causes—which can be many.

Improper diet and emotional worries are the worst offenders. If you rule these out, consider (1) coffee and tea (in excess); (2) tobacco; (3) alcohol; (4) drugs.

Over many centuries, man has used various herbs, "love potions," stimulants, and narcotics in his search for happiness and tranquility. Discuss with your doctor whether you have become a slave to some of the energy detractors mentioned above.

COFFEE AND TEA

The active ingredient in coffee is caffeine and this drug is found also in tea, although a cup of tea contains only about 60 percent as much as a cup of coffee. Evidence suggests that coffee in moderation improves the speed and accuracy of muscular work as well as of mental work. When coffee is taken alone it is more effective in bringing about those benefits than when taken with meals. The results wear off quickly, however, but apparently leave no ill effects. When you are faced with a tough task you are justified in taking coffee in small quantities to make you more fit to undertake it. The same can be said of tea.

However, scientific findings indicate that coffee *in excess*—five or more cups per day—can be harmful. Research suggests that excess is a factor in heart disease, poor job performance, ringing in the ears, severe anxiety, and other psychiatric disorders. (Caffeine is also an ingredient in some headache tablets and cola drinks, which must therefore be counted as equivalents of cups of coffee.)

Symptoms of over-caffeinization may be insomnia, hallucinations, headaches, irritability, nausea, irregular heartbeat, and shortness of breath. Quite a list! Decaffeinated coffee avoids the jitters, but provides less pick-me-up.

Caffeine (coffee, tea, cola) in moderation, then, can be helpful; in excess, harmful.

TOBACCO

All available scientific evidence suggests that the use of tobacco undermines working efficiency. A comprehensive study made by Johns Hopkins University discovered that 54 percent of those who smoke over 10 cigarettes per day die before the age of 60; against this, only 43 percent of nonsmokers die before that age. Among the harmful effects ascribable to smoking are a stimulation of the adrenal glands; increase in sugar from the liver; increase in irritability; a drainage of nerve energy; acid stomach; headaches; irritated linings of the nose, throat, and lungs. Smokers treble their chances of having a heart attack. Smoking is the greatest single cause of lung cancer.

Despite warnings from the U.S. Surgeon General's Office, about 40 percent of adults continue to smoke. You will have to decide for yourself whether the benefits you feel you get from smoking are worth more to you than the risks in health and personal effectiveness.

Some time ago I saw a TV program on emphysema which showed photographs of the lungs of nonsmokers and of heavy smokers. If I hadn't stopped smoking many years ago, I believe those photographs would have made me quit on the spot!

ALCOHOL CAN BECOME YOUR BOSS

Alcohol is a depressant, not a stimulant. Even in small quantities such as those found in beer or light wine, it will cause a loss of effectiveness in memory, of judgment, and of all thinking processes. Moreover, it tends to cause loss of control of muscular activity, as to both speed and accuracy. The fact that an individual *thinks* he has reasoned better or worked better after taking a drink or two is merely testimony that he has thought less clearly; it cannot stand up against the testimony of laboratory findings.

Studies have shown that daily imbibing of three martinis, or the equivalent, resulted in severe damage to the liver, heart, and brain; impaired memory; and deterioration in the structure of muscles.

Inasmuch as alcohol obviously tends to loosen inhibitions, however, there is something to be said for it as a lubricant for social contacts. But if you indulge in a few drinks for conviviality's sake, do so with the full knowledge that your system must absorb the effects. If you drink, do so in great moderation, never to excess, and try to eat some protein food along with the drinking. Never take a drink in the hope that it will help you to solve some mental or physical task which you anticipate will be difficult. It will not. If you do drink, you are likely to be an inane conversationalist and a lousy listener.

There is no attempt here to sermonize about the use of alcohol. It is recognized that in our modern life the price the body must pay for absorbing alcohol may occasionally be warranted by the social benefits yielded. However, every reader should understand clearly that the regular use of alcohol, or the occasional use of alcohol in excess, is a great deterrent to personal effectiveness and provides a shortened route to the undertaker.

DRUGS

Many Americans are drug addicts and don't know it. What's more, they won't believe it. Pain, which is nature's warning that something is wrong, we feel must be killed or suppressed at all costs. Yet drugs to stop pain may do more harm than the ailment which is causing the pain.

Most readers, when discussing drug addiction, think in terms of habit-forming cocaine, heroin, LSD (acid) or marijuana (pot, grass). Cocaine, basically a pain reliever, is a stimulant which can cause hallucinations. Heroin (and the less strong morphine) comes from the poppy plant and is a highly addictive drug that dulls the senses and induces sleep. LSD is a dangerous drug which leads to recurring hallucinations. Marijuana brings on a state of euphoria—gaiety, excitement or amusement.

Cocaine, heroin, morphine, and LSD are classed as "hard drugs" and are dangerous in lay hands. Unfortunately, many people think they can take other *narcotics* on their own. Narcotics are classed as either stimulants or depressants. Young addicts call them "uppers" or "downers." Many a medicine chest contains benzedrine (a stimulant), or barbiturates (sleeping pills and sedatives), which are depressants. People who "must have" some form of narcotic are addicts, even if they won't admit it. The victim will suffer agony if the drug is withheld. Moreover, his body builds up a tolerance to a given drug, so that ever larger doses are demanded. Unless hospitalized and cured, drug addicts become emotionally imbalanced, may become criminals to feed their habit, and most certainly will severely shorten their lives.

People who feel unworthy, guilty, fearful, lonely, depressed, or inferior fall easy prey to drugs. If you're hooked on alcohol, tobacco, or drugs of any sort, take heed!

SLEEP FOR RENEWED ENERGY

In the previous chapter we considered the role of sleep in relaxation. Additionally, sleep restores energy and sometimes fosters subconscious resolution of problems which have eluded rational thought.

The millions of our body cells undergo repair during sleep. Muscles get rid of fatigue poisons that have accumulated from use;

even the heart muscle gets some rest by virtue of beating more slowly. Breathing is also slower as well as deeper. Body temperature and basal metabolism rates fall slightly. Digestion continues to absorb needed nutrients.

Sound sleep regenerates and reinvigorates. (However, studies at the University of California revealed that too much sleep—10 hours or more—can leave you "dopey" for four or five hours after waking, unless the long sleep is making up for lost sleep or great fatigue.) Many people regularly short-change themselves on sleep, awakening tired and irritable—stress which leads to more stress and depletion of energy. Fatigue piles up cumulatively, drops sharply with rest. If the rest interruption is missing, day after day, there's trouble ahead.

If you have trouble falling asleep, try drinking a glass of warm milk before retiring. The Maryland Psychiatric Research Center reports that milk contains an amino acid (L-tryptophane) which induces sleep. It's a lot safer than drugs.

FEEL TIRED MOST OF THE TIME?

Maybe you wake up just as tired as when you went to bed—or find it an effort to drag yourself around all day long.

That feeling of fatigue may be nature's way of telling you something's wrong. Here are some of the possible causes:

1. Vitamin or mineral deficiencies (see Chapter 5).
2. Unusual physical *over*exertion, such as experienced by the accountant, say, who plays strenuous weekend tennis and feels "dead tired" on Mondays (see Chapter 4).
3. Heavy, continuing but usual physical activity, such as that experienced by stevedores or furniture movers. This kind of heavy labor uses up reserves of oxygen and blood sugar ten times as fast as mild activity—faster than the body can replace them. Fatigue "piles up" if rest is denied.
4. Unresolved emotional conflict, long endured (see Chapter 12).
5. Prolonged mental work. Your active brain requires one-seventh of the body's blood flow, almost one-quarter of your oxygen intake and a continuous supply of blood sugar. If these supplies are endangered, the brain slows down the activity of other blood-demanding organs (i.e., you feel tired).

There are various ways to overcome fatigue, some good, some not so good. Nature's way is rest and sleep. If diet is proper, and worry is absent, this solution is the best by far. A physician well versed in nutrition can track down any dietary deficiencies. Much of this book is devoted to helping you conquer emotional imbalance, if that's the cause of your fatigue.

Alcohol? Tobacco? Sleeping pills, pep pills, relaxers? Coffee? Coca Cola? Candy? These are temporary palliatives at best, and may be dangerous or habit-forming, as we have noted. Slack off on them.

If you are chronically tired, can't seem to get ahead of it, you will be wise to get a thorough physical examination. Listen to your body—it possesses a life-granting wisdom.

To the above five causes of tiredness, let us add a sixth: boredom. The increase in leisure time for most of us has greatly contributed to boredom. Absence of inner interest or outer stimulation are principal characteristics. What strikes one person as tedious, challenges another; therefore, some folks can label as "boring" any particular job, activity, or situation. Conversely, we cannot label an individual as "bore-prone" because he is disinterested in specific things, matters, or subjects.

Persons dependent on outside stimulation are more liable to boredom than those who depend on inner resources—thought and imagination. The former must find bigger and better "kicks"; the latter welcomes time for contemplation.

If you are bored, take on some different activity, or challenge; pioneer a new adventure; find an unselfish way to serve others; take up a new game or sport which requires physical action. Variety is the spice of life, runs an old adage.

Figure 7, "How Much 'Pep' Do I Have?," gives you an opportunity to evaluate ten factors which can contribute to, or detract from, your energy.

FIGURE 7
How much "pep" do I have?

In each of the ten lines below, check the block which comes closest to your self-appraisal. If you can't decide between two blocks, check the narrow space between them. Be honest, but not harsh with yourself!

Factor	2	3	4	5	6	7	8	9	10
Nutrition	I eat and drink many sweets		I pay no attention to my diet		I eat what is served me		I think I get a balanced diet		I have made a study of nutrition
Sunshine	Artificial light most of the time		Sunshine on weekends principally		I get some every day		I get at least an hour every day		Regular and plentiful sunshine
Play	I have no opportunity for play		Taking time to play doesn't interest me		Generally I accept invitations to play		I jump at chances to play		I plan and get regular recreation
Sleep	I suffer from insomnia		I'm awake a lot		Usually I get enough		I sleep quite soundly		Feel full of pep when I awake
Endurance	I'm tired most of the time		I'm easily fatigued		I enjoy a fair, normal endurance		Seldom tire under prolonged effort		I seem to be almost tireless
Anxiety	I'm torn apart with worry		I worry a great deal		I suffer occasional anxiety		I believe most things work out for the best		I'm at peace with my lot in life
Hate	I strongly hate one or more persons		I resent a few people		I get occasional spells		I feel friendly toward most people		Mostly I'm loving and friendly
Fear	I'm afraid of many things and people		I'm timid, I guess		I have a few fears		I have sufficient courage		I honestly fear nothing or no one
Guilt	I'm burdened with a strong secret guilt		I have annoying guilt feelings		I try to brush off feelings of guilt		I've risen above any guilt feelings		There are no guilts to oppress me
Attitude	I live in an unfair world		I'm inclined to pessimism		Occasionally I get "down"		I'm optimistic about most things		I'm happy with life

5

"Tell me what you eat and..."

"Tell me what you eat, and I'll tell you what you are," is a slogan with much truth in it. Nutrition can affect not only your daily living level but also your long-time health and energy. Well-balanced nutrition can make you cheerful, full of pep, clear-headed, adjusted; poor nutrition can cause you to be irritable, lazy, mentally sluggish and hostile to your environment.

WHAT IS A CALORIE?

A calorie is a unit of heat: the amount of heat needed to raise one gram of water (about 1/30th of an ounce) one degree Centigrade (which is 1.8 times a degree Fahrenheit, the scale to which Americans are accustomed).

One calorie is a small amount. It takes several hundred of these small calories to raise a pint of water 1° F. Hence, a unit of 1,000 small calories is used, called a K-cal, when talking about food calories.

Such a calorie means that when a measured amount of food is "burned" in the body, it releases the stated number of calories available as energy. For example, a normal slice of bread provides 60 to 100 calories, an egg, 70 to 80, a sweetened cola drink, 130 to 140, one quarter pound of beef, sauteed with oil, about 250.

Some calories are needed just to sustain your body functions (basal metabolism). How many will depend on your weight. Additional calories needed will depend on how physically or mentally active you are.

Children need about 2,000 calories per day, adult males, 3,000. Older folks require fewer calories per pound of weight than young adults.

PROTEINS, BUILDING BLOCKS OF TISSUE

Protein is found in many forms in your body—it's in muscles, red blood corpuscles, infection-fighting antibodies in the blood-stream, and in enzymes which accelerate digestion and many bodily changes.

Muscles which have not been supplied with adequate protein lose elasticity, which may contribute to poor posture. Since hair and fingernails are largely protein, they too will suffer. Fortunately, proper diet can reverse these conditions within a few weeks.

There are other protein-deficiency situations which are not so readily corrected: anemia, low blood pressure, morning sluggishness, fatigue, resistance to infections, inadequate digestion and water-logged tissues.

Protein is supplied in abundance by meat, poultry, fish, eggs, milk and cheese. Other sources are bread, cereal, peanuts, dry beans and soybeans. At times eggs have come under attack as a cause of increasing blood cholesterol levels. Studies of persons with normal blood pressure and cholesterol fail to support this apprehension. But if you already have a cholesterol problem, you will be wise to follow your physician's advice as to egg consumption.

CABROHYDRATES FOR ENERGY

Carbohydrates are starches and sugars. Principally, they supply your energy. Starches are supplied by wheat, corn, oats, rice, potatoes, sweet potatoes, and vegetables such as soybeans, peanuts, peas, and dry beans. Sugars are supplied by refined and unrefined sugar, molasses, honey, and many fruits.

Sugar is one of 40 or more nutrients essential to health. In over-supply it can be harmful; in undersupply it can lead to hunger, weakness, irritability, headaches, and fatigue.

Breakfast is your most important meal, for it pretty well determines your energy for the coming day. When it includes protein and some fat, sugars are absorbed more slowly and hence energy remains at a high level longer. Nutritionists say, "Breakfast like a king, lunch like a prince, dinner like a pauper."

Energy results from the "burning" (oxydizing) of sugar, or sugar and fat together. When three meals high in carbohydrates are eaten, excessive demands are made upon the pancreas for insulin; oddly enough, fatigue, rather than energy, results.

Starches are readily converted to sugar; and sugar can be stored as glycogen, to be reconverted to sugar as demanded by physical activity.

Americans tend to get too much starch and sugar in their diets—especially refined (white) sugar. From childhood on we consume excessive amounts of candy, jam, soft drinks, sweetened cereals, cake, pies, cookies, rich desserts, canned fruits, and ice cream. Cut your intake of them by 90 percent and you may be amazed by the difference in the way you feel.

Sugar is a necessary nutrient, but in excess it may be stored as unwanted fat. There are a half-dozen forms of sugar (sucrose, fructose, glucose, etc.) which have different rates of digestive absorption. Since these nutrients are found in fruits, milk, many vegetables, meats and seafoods it is highly desirable to lessen the direct intake of sweets and starches. You don't really need those starchy foods and sweet desserts.

FATS ARE NECESSARY, TOO

Fats, like carbohydrates, provide energy and yield basic elements of body cells. Fat also protects many vital organs by providing a cushion around them. Fats are supplied principally by butter, margarine, shortening, cream, some cheeses, vegetable oils (corn, soybean, cottonseed and safflower), mayonnaise, bacon, egg yolk, meats and nuts.

Fat is burned most efficiently when some sugar is also present. Sugar can be changed into (an inadequate) fat, but fat cannot be changed into sugar. When fats are broken down in the digestive process, glycerol and various fatty acids are formed—some are essential to life. Hence, no-fat, or extremely low-fat, diets can invite trouble, easily correctible by taking several teaspoonsful of vegetable oils (daily). By a strange quirk, complete avoidance of vegetable oils can contribute to obesity.

Fats soon turn rancid; hydrogenation prevents rancidity but destroys much nutritive value. Hence vegetable fats in their natural state are preferable. These come from corn, soybean, and cotton-seed oils used in salad dressings and from nuts or fresh-ground peanut butter, *unhydrogenated*. Animal fats should be taken in limited amounts only, and most fried foods should be avoided.

A "polyunsaturated" fat is capable of absorbing additional hydrogen and is usually a liquid oil from some vegetable source. Taken in quantity, it tends to lower the amount of cholesterol in the blood, and hence to avoid heart attacks and strokes.

A "saturated" fat is not capable of absorbing more hydrogen, and usually comes from meat, egg yolks, butter, and other animal products. Eaten to excess, these foods add to the cholesterol which the body itself manufactures, causing a narrowing (atherosclerosis) of the coronary (and other) arteries.

MINERALS

Your body demands an amazing variety of minerals. Some of these minerals exist in minute amounts and are called trace minerals. Great deficiencies in any one mineral will ultimately reveal itself as some abnormal condition.

Calcium and supportive phosphorous mostly reside in bones and teeth. Phosphorous also lodges in muscles and soft tissue. These two elements, plus iron, are often deficient. All three are important for proper functioning of the heart and circulatory system.

Calcium is supplied by milk, cheese, and dark green, leafy vege-tables; iron by liver, heart, kidneys, lean meats, shellfish, whole grains and the leafy vegetables like collards, mustard greens and turnip greens.

Another essential element, iodine, is supplied by seafoods or iodized salt. Many foods supply sodium, potassium (bananas are a good source), magnesium, zinc and copper. A varied diet will generally supply adequate amounts of minerals.

IRON DEFICIENCY

Some individuals absorb food-supplied iron inefficiently, resulting in deficiency in the quality of red blood cells. Some physical signs are facial pallor and paleness in the red color of the corners of the eyes, the gums, and mucous membranes of the mouth. Lassitude and easy fatigue are usually present, along with irritability and vague aches and pains.

Oral doses of medicinal iron will usually correct this type of anemia quite readily. If oral ingestion causes gastric cramps or diarrhea, your physician can inject iron intravenously—but first he will make certain that your anemic tendency is not due to some other cause.

VITAMINS

A varied food intake normally supplies the dozen or more vitamins your body needs. Here are the principal vitamins, the roles they play in body chemistry, and some good sources for them.

Vitamin A helps the skin and mucous membranes resist infection and is important to good eyesight. It is supplied by liver, kidney, whole milk (or fortified skim milk), peaches, apricots, cantaloupes, and papayas, deep yellow and dark green vegetables. The fruits and vegetables mentioned do not directly supply vitamin A; instead, they supply carotene which the body converts to the vitamin. (Excessive doses of vitamin A can be harmful rather than helpful.)

Various B vitamins mysteriously support one another. Deficiency of B_1 (thiamin) contributes to sluggishness, depression, irritability, forgetfulness, sleeplessness, fatigue, constipation, low blood pressure, anemia, heart irregularity, and neuritis. Most of these symptoms soon disappear when adequate (not excessive) B_1 is supplied. Foods rich in B_1 are wheat germ, whole grain cereals, nuts, dry beans, peas, soybeans, lentils, pork, heart and kidneys.

Deficiency of B_2 (riboflavin) shows itself as a purplish tongue, cracks in lips and corners of mouth, eyes sensitive to light, bloodshot eyes, and visible capillaries in the cheeks, under the eyes.

Another B vitamin, pantothenic acid, is supplied in milk, yogurt, liver, yeast, and cooked leafy vegetables. Older persons often report improved eyesight when this vitamin is in adequate supply.

B_6 insufficiency causes headaches, dizziness, lethargy, irritability and skin problems. The deficiency can be corrected by taking yeast, blackstrap molasses, wheat bran and germ, liver, heart, and kidney. Certain individuals seem to require large amounts of B_6.

B_{12} offsets anemic tendencies, especially if taken in conjunction with folic acid. Milk, cheese, eggs, liver, yeast, nuts, and green vegetables are indicated foods.

All B vitamins dissolve in water and cannot be stored in the body. Since they function as a team, loading up with one only increases the need for the others. Since whole grain breads and cereals are largely missing from our diets (because of overprocessing), the best sources of B vitamins as a group are wheat germ, brewers yeast, and liver. Supplementary capsules of B complex can help; usually they also contain important minerals.

Vitamin C (ascorbic acid) prevents scurvy, and strengthens various connective tissues such as cartilage, ligaments, and walls of bloodvessels. The best sources are citrus fruits, tomato juice, cabbage, and strawberries.

Sunlight, calcium and strong bones go together. If you fail to get sufficient exposure to sunlight, the vitamin can be supplied by cod liver oil or by vitamin D-enriched milk. Excessive sunlight ages the skin and can cause skin cancers. Likewise, excessive intake of D capsules can cause trouble.

Vitamin E is said to slow the aging process. It can be supplied by wheat germ and unprocessed whole wheat. It is most effective if vitamin C is taken at the same time. Injections of PABA (para-amino benzoic acid) have also been credited with reversing the aging process. (See section on vitamin E below, "How about Vitamin E?)

Vitamin K helps blood to clot. It is produced by intestinal bacteria which benefit from yogurt, milk, and unsaturated fatty acids (vegetable oils).

If you consistently follow a varied diet, you may not need supplementary vitamins. However, since vitamins can be lost in storage, cooking, and processing, you may wish to play it safe by taking a multiple vitamin and mineral capsule each day.

HOW ABOUT VITAMIN E?

Vitamin E proponents assert that massive doses help prevent heart attacks or restore your body to normal if you have an attack. They say that European doctors use vitamin E widely, in diseases of infancy and old age.

Opponents remain unconvinced. They admit that E is essential, but say that its role in the human body has not been discovered. They suggest, moreover, that an adequate diet (vegetables, vegetable oils, milk, wheat germ, lean meat, eggs, and fruit) will supply all the vitamin E your body can use.

When medical experts disagree, you and I are disadvantaged. So my suggestion is to do as I am doing—read all you can on this subject from authoritative sources, hoping that the controversy will be resolved one way or the other.

ROUGHAGE IN YOUR DIET

Malignancy of the colon and rectum will strike more than 100,000 Americans annually, kill half of them, and handicap the daily life of the remainder. In the undeveloped countries of Africa the incidence of such cancer is about 7 percent of the U.S. rate. The percentage increases as natives move to cities and adopt westernized, "bland" diets.

Diet is the villain. It is believed that lack of roughage foods is largely responsible. American foods are subjected to too much processing, or to dangerous additives, so that carcinogenic (cancer-inducing) substances remain in the intestines longer than they should. Bulk (roughage, fibrous) foods speed up the process of food passage, even though they themselves are partially indigestible. There are other values in a high roughage diet. It causes you to chew longer, producing more saliva, which swells the bulk in the stomach and so decreases interest in more food. You will excrete more fat, and avoid constipation. Other diseases are also related to an insufficient roughage diet. Among these are diverticulosis (pouches in the colon), appendicitis, and possibly certain heart conditions.

You can add roughage to your diet by eating *whole grain* cereals

and bread, bran, wheat germ, raw vegetables, and brown rice. Bran
is highly concentrated fiber. Two heaping spoonsful a day will do
wonders for your elimination.

DRINKING WATER

Some communities have tap water which is dangerous to health,
or unpalatable. Even some of the chemicals used to combat pollution can be harmful. Ask the city fathers of your community for a
statement of water purity. If you are dubious, consider bottled or
distilled water, or merely filtered water. Finally, see to it that you
drink six to eight glasses of water every day of your life, most of it
not with your meals.

FASTING

Fasting—simply doing without food for a number of days—can
have some benign effects, but has attendant risks. Authorities say
that it can: (1) burn up excess fat; (2) lower high blood pressure;
(3) rid the body of harmful toxins (waste materials); (4) reduce the
size of your swollen stomach and hence lessen your body's demand
for future overeating. Dr. Ragnar Berg, a Nobel Prize recipient, says
that under fasting, diseased tissues in the body are the first to be
broken down in order to meet its nutritive needs, so contributing
to healing.

In fasting, there is first a loss of water stored in tissues, as well
as a loss of sodium and potassium. Increasingly, the body uses up
glycogen from the liver, then begins to break down protein from
the muscles. Then it uses up substances (ketones) resulting from
breakdown of body fat. The breaking-down process (catabolism)
puts a heavy burden on liver and kidneys, altering the production
of insulin and other important substances. Vitamins and minerals
are lost, but not replaced. Obviously, fasting cannot be pursued too
long.

Since half of those who undertake fasting soon regain their
weight loss, sensible calorie intake, balanced diet, and exercise are
the preferred method of weight reduction.

Since there are dangers in fasting, or even in dieting, you should
not undertake either without supervision from a nutritionally-

oriented physician. For some individuals (with diabetes, tuberculosis, or cancer, for example) fasting is extremely inadvisable.

EATING RIGHT

Good eating habits can improve both health and the family budget. Here are tips from nutritionists:

1. Your evening meal should be the lightest of the three.
2. Regularly include in your diet lean meat or fish, skimmed milk or yogurt, cheese, margarine, vegetable oil, wholemeal flour products, fruits and vegetables (leafy, green, yellow), cabbage, roughage.
3. Consume only small quantities of bread, other white flour products, potatoes, sugar, sweet desserts, alcohol, fat meats, butter, *whole* milk, ice cream, coffee, and condiments.
4. Chew food slowly to allow ptyalin in saliva to break down starches and facilitate digestion in the stomach.
5. When digestion is thorough, you need less food. Most Americans consume two to three times more than their bodies require, causing extra weight or indigestion.
6. Avoid eating when you are under tension; be relaxed during and after eating.

6

Become a social being

Some folks need to rejoin the human race. Turtle-like, they have withdrawn into their shells, occasionally sticking their necks out timidly.

This chapter and the next will point out the many success values to you in relating well to others.

YOUR SOCIAL DEVELOPMENT

Success, if measured in terms of cold dollars and cents, can frequently be achieved by direct action such as technical education, burning ambition, high activity, long hours, and ruthlessness. However, money success often comes to those who do not follow the hard paths, but who are more concerned in giving than in getting. If you gauge success in terms of the esteem of your fellow men, rather than in terms of material possessions, then most certainly it will result from the expression of your energy in social contacts. It will be not so much what you know that will be important, but what you do. Success will come not so much from education, important though that is, as from your social development—something you cannot get merely from books.

"Extroversion" is the term frequently applied to individuals who are gregarious and get along well with their fellows. The opposite of this is "introversion" and the two terms mean turning outward (extroversion) and turning inward (introversion). We hear these terms used frequently, and you may erroneously get the impression that an individual must be one or the other. This is decidedly not the case, for at least 50 percent of us would have to be classed as "ambiverts," which might be defined as turning two ways. As a matter of fact, no individual is so extrovert that he never exhibits introvert tendencies; conversely, no individual is so introvert that he never exhibits extrovert tendencies. We can class an individual as either extrovert or introvert depending upon the predominance of his social reactions. If most of the time he responds in a typically extrovert manner, we call that person an extrovert. If, on the other hand, most of the time he exhibits typical introvert reactions, we call him an introvert. If he manifests extrovert and introvert traits in approximately equal degree, he would be classed as an ambivert.

Individuals are not extrovert or introvert by heredity. Native endowment does not limit one's ability to become extrovert as, for example, it limits his ultimate typing speed. Extroversion and introversion are largely matters of developed social habits. Those who are socially intelligent are those who have developed good social patterns of habit response to human contacts. Those who have developed less adequate responses are said to possess less social intelligence, or are said to be introvert.

Interests in things are likely to be extroverting, since they fasten attention outside of self. Typical would be gardening, mechanical construction, participation in sports, certain hobbies. However, since many of these activities can be performed alone, they are usually less extroverting than activities involving other people.

Before we go too far, let us note some of the characteristics manifested by those who are classed as introverts and extroverts.

INTROVERTS VERSUS EXTROVERTS

The true introvert is introspective and imaginative. His energies turn inward and many of them are unexpressed in action. Often he is an excellent student. He builds dream castles but, because he is afraid of making mistakes or of becoming embarrassed, does little to carry them out. Usually he will avoid personal conflicts, but tends to take the easy way out of such situations. Frequently he avoids meeting people, or carrying out obligations which are expected of him by other members of his group. He has many thoughts as to the good deeds he would like to do. He avoids doing those things which he dislikes, yet suffers many emotional upsets. He would rather write reports than deliver talks, craves praise, may be caustic, is sensitive to criticism, rebels at discipline and, if creative, works as an individualist. In group contact he tends to take the easiest way out of each situation, but in the end he pays many penalties, because he yearns for human companionship, feels slighted at minor rebuffs, and finds himself unable to adjust to the give and take of life.

The extrovert, of course, is opposite of the above. He is objective, not subjective. He may be careless as to dress, outspoken, open to criticism, not highly sensitive or imaginative. His extrovert social habits, however, are built by difficult endeavor, and do not just spring into existence. For example, he accepts office in a club, or does his best to make a speech, or sacrifices amusement time to help someone. As he progresses in these things he finds himself becoming stronger. He is less likely to read ulterior meanings which were not intended; he accepts criticism as something constructive and of use to him; he finds personal satisfaction in doing, not merely in thinking about doing; he doesn't need praise so badly, because he has the joy of performance; he finds the good in others; he finds unexpected rewards for his extrovert acts and becomes convinced of their usefulness.

The extrovert projects his thoughts and actions outward for others, and the introvert refers outward actions to himself. You may, however, do an extrovert thing one minute and an introvert thing the next minute. The usual way you respond comes to be characteristic of you.

Figure 8 contrasts the life curves of two individuals. The influences of school life and marriage are indicated. Note how the early extrovert habits of *A* cause him to be extrovert most of his adult life. Individual *B*, on the other hand, fails to achieve any such level of outgoingness.

VALUES OF EXTROVERSION

The introvert usually takes the easy way out of social contacts and obligations, only to suffer in the long run through lack of

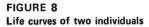

FIGURE 8
Life curves of two individuals

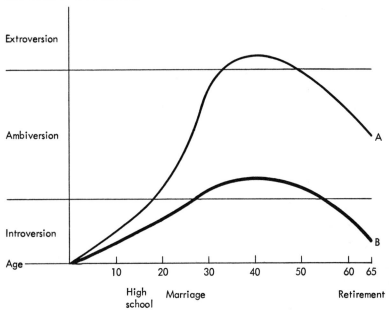

human warmth and friendliness. The extrovert, on the other hand, usually struggles to build up social habits which bind him closer to others so that in the long run he has many friends and much human warmth as his reward.

You can look back on your own life and recall instances where introvert acts on your part caused losses of friendship or of happiness, whereas extrovert acts on your part resulted in pleasant memories which linger and glow. The chances are high that right now you are an ambivert, displaying a mixture of extrovert and introvert social habits. If you want an interesting contrast, list the last five activities which you did which represent extrovert acts— acts leading outward from you toward people, to improve their happiness, to make them like you, and to work with them cooperatively. Then list the last five introvert acts you have done— acts where you withdrew from social contact, or took umbrage where it was unintended, or refused to meet someone halfway.

What could you have done with the latter five to make them extrovert? What will you do with them in the future if they come up again?

Particularly when others are under stress will your extrovert acts be well received. If you take care of your neighbors' children the day they move into a new house they will remember it much longer than any of the other days when you watched over their children. Help—in a tight place—is double help.

Marriage is one of the great extroverting influences of life, for it causes each mate to think and do for the welfare of other members of the family. Introversion is the unseen ghost at many a divorce proceeding. Research has repeatedly confirmed that divorced people are more introvert than those happily married; that those unhappily married are more introvert than those happily married; that those who succeed in any line of endeavor are more likely to be extrovert than those who are mediocre or who fail in that endeavor. We could almost set up a principle: extroversion aids success and happiness in any line.

Let us apply this principle to you as an individual. Read the following sentence carefully: "If I become more extrovert, I increase my chances of success in business, in marriage and in friendships."

That sentence is important. Please go back and read it aloud. Memorize it. Let it become a guiding rule for you in social contact. Bring it to mind each time you are asked to take on some social obligation, or to join a group, or to give a talk, or to listen to criticism. Cast thy bread upon the waters, and it will come back to you—buttered.

ANALYSIS OF EXTROVERSION-INTROVERSION

Is introversion always undesirable, and extroversion always desirable?

There are three areas in which introversion-extroversion can be noted: intellectual, social, and emotional. Some characteristics of the various combinations are shown on page 71.

You can be extrovert in one area, ambivert or introvert in the other two—or other combinations. This fact makes possible precise thinking—no longer need you generalize, "He's an introvert person."

Area	Extrovert	Ambivert	Introvert
Intellectual	Executes plans Writes well Voluble Large vocabulary Dislikes routine work	Sometimes extrovert, sometimes introvert	Overly imaginative Dislikes writing things Uncommunicative Small vocabulary Likes routine work
Social	Likes to be with people Likes center of stage Strong sense of dramatic Wears flashy clothes Careless about possessions Lends things freely Gives praise	Sometimes extrovert, sometimes introvert	Likes to be alone Is retiring Self-effacing Wears conservative clothes Very orderly Is fussy about possessions Craves praise
Emotional	"Blows up" easily May be a "cry baby" Is demonstrative Laughs aloud Talks in a loud voice Is uninhibited	Sometimes extrovert, sometimes introvert	Is a "stoic" Stands pain well Is undemonstrative Rarely laughs Uses subdued voice Seems repressed

Instead, you now may conclude, "He's an intellectual introvert, a social extrovert, an emotional ambivert." Since the way you handle extroverts and introverts differs, such analytic observation on your part will help you in human relations.

It is normally true that extrovert traits are more desirable than introvert traits. But extremes of both are annoying. The extreme extrovert intellectually, may want to show his superior knowledge; socially, may seek the limelight, be overzealous; emotionally, may be unstable.

The extreme introvert on the other hand intellectually, may be uninteresting; socially, may be shy, sensitive and retiring; emotionally, may seem callous.

Study yourself, and the kind of work you do, to determine whether you should increase, or decrease, some of your present traits.

TOLERANCE

Tolerance is one form of extroversion, and is also a sign of a mature personality. It can even be classed as a valuable social skill.

Your childhood, education, social contacts and experiences ultimately equip you with certain information and emotional sets, or

72

attitudes. Others with different backgrounds, aims, customs and standards develop different ideas and attitudes. Frequently, yours and theirs are influenced by traditions, race, nationality, religion, politics and similar influences. When attitudes come into conflict, which one is right, which wrong? The opinionated man says, "I am right." The tolerant man says, "It is not a question of right or wrong—only that they are different. Let's first find out how much they have in common, then consider the differences."

Each of us constructs the walls of his own psychic house, within which he must think, feel, decide. If it is a tiny house, there will be no room for others: he will be cocksure, intolerant. Here are some characteristics of an intolerant person: hypercritical, belittling, nagging, prejudiced, hostile, cynical, suspicious, quick to take offense, intimidating, exploiting, power-lustful, contempt for softness or compromise or reconciliation. He is emotionally fettered by his own intolerance.

Let's consider his direct opposite. He tries to marshall the positive energies of those he encounters. With quiet words and friendly deeds he lowers the psychic barriers between himself and those of varying views or cultures. He displays understanding, compassion, appreciation, affection, humility, empathy.

How about you—do you make psychic room for the other fellow?

YOUR PERSONALITY DEVELOPMENT

There is nothing so small as a man wrapped up in himself. We hear much talk about personality as though it were some God-given attribute. Somehow or other we tend to associate personality and good looks, or personality and neat dress. Good looks do not make personality, although improvement in personality will tend to improve personal appearance and there are sound physiological reasons in support of this statement. However, we all know individuals of whom we say, "Oh, she is not at all good-looking, but everybody likes her." This is but another way of saying that she has an excellent personality.

No matter what your stage of personality development, you can improve it tremendously by developing good social habits. As an example of what is meant by good social habits note this list:

1. Develop anew the genuine smile.
2. Become interested in people as individuals, in their hopes and aspirations.
3. Be a good listener. Get people to talk about the things they want to talk about.
4. Praise when praise is due.
5. Don't take your friends and loved ones for granted; tell them the things which you appreciate about them.
6. Do small acts for others without expectation of benefit to yourself.
7. Observe the minor courtesies.
8. Speak well of others behind their backs. Speak ill of no one.
9. Refrain from gossip or scandalmongering.
10. Take active part in the discussions and activities of groups to which you belong.
11. Look for some good in everyone—it's there.
12. Talk about positive things and avoid the negative.

To acquire social development, you must practice good social habits. It is not enough to *know* that you should smile graciously; you must smile graciously or affably when the proper situation arises. If you are going to learn to say thank you, the only way to do it is to thank people when it is due them. If you are going to learn to praise or show appreciation or to be tactful or to speak well of others, the only way you can build these habits is by practicing them at opportune occasions.

Look for those occasions; they are all around you. Within the next hour there may be several such opportunities. Don't let them slip by. Psychology gives ample substantiation for the philosophy which says, "Assume a virtue if you have it not." Assume the virtues of extroversion and soon you will have them for your very own.

EXERCISE YOUR PERSONALITY

Whatever your present personality development, you can improve it by proper exercise. Your personality is the sum total of your physical, mental, social, and emotional powers. Each power can be developed by using it, exercising it; on the other hand, each one can atrophy from disuse or be wrecked by abuse. Deterioration in one can tend to tear down the others.

It is important to use properly each one of the four powers. Actually, they reinforce one another—good health facilitates mental work, good emotions make for good health, good social relations yield positive emotions, etc. By consciously developing your powers, you *exercise your personality.*

When a number of large corporations were queried as to the traits that they considered most important to employee success, 70 percent of them answered "the ability to get along with people." And the Carnegie Institute, after studying records of 10,000 employees, concluded that 15 percent of success is due to technical training and 85 percent to personality development.

Social ability is one of the important aspects of personality development. Yet it is largely a matter of forming the proper social habits. The right habits need to be formed and practiced, the wrong habits replaced.

> I know a man who has built an excellent social habit. Each time he learns something good about an acquaintance, he drops him a short note of congratulation. If he sees a newspaper item of interest to an acquaintance he clips it, and mails it. Everybody speaks well of that man; he is frequently elected to office in groups to which he belongs; and he has a host of admiring friends—like me.

Similar social habits are telephoning to keep in touch with acquaintances; visiting them, especially when they are lonely or in sorrow; joining with others in worthwhile movements; active participation in group activities; praising others for their accomplishments; showing friendliness by both deed and word.

Exercising social habits makes it easier to do them again and again.

ARE YOU A GOOD JUDGE OF CHARACTER?

Most of us think we're pretty savvy when it comes to sizing people up. Largely on external signs, we conclude that some new acquaintance is a lion or mouse, intelligent or dumb, stolid or temperamental, sickly or healthy. Even hostility at a first encounter may not be permanently indicative, may merely reflect some misconception or be the backwash of some prior happening.

Here are some suggestions to guide you in passing judgments about people you know only casually:

1. Avoid preconceived generalizations: all redheads have bad tempers; all fat people are jolly, etc.
2. The surrounding circumstance may influence the other person's behavior.
3. Defects may be obvious to you, but additionally look for the good points.
4. Reserve judgment until you have had a number of contacts, preferably under different conditions.
5. Listen. Don't do most of the talking. Ask questions but don't probe.
6. He wants to be understood, as do you. Help the process.

MASLOW'S HIERARCHY OF NEEDS

Dr. Abraham Maslow developed the hierarchy of needs (see Figure 9). In essence, his well-accepted theory says that human needs fall into five levels, running from physiological needs for

FIGURE 9
Maslow's hierarchy of needs

Creativity; use of unique aptitudes; personal fulfillment	Self-realization
Recognition; self-esteem; status; reputation	Ego
Belonging; acceptance; conformity; friendship; love	Social
Security against natural forces, deprivations, and persons	Safety
Food, water, air, sex, rest, sleep, physical activity	Physiological

Shaded portion shows estimated percentage of needs satisfied by the average person.

survival to the highest level of self-actualization, which rather few of us ever satisfy. A study of Figure 9 will give you a good idea of the components of each level.

When an individual is able to achieve most, or all, the constituents at a given level, he begins to seek satisfactions at higher levels. (We see the same force at work in the aspirations of most developing nations.) This shifting of demand to ever higher levels will explain why employees don't show gratitude when insurance benefits are improved, or your wife wants to take an art course soon after you've bought her all those modern labor-saving appliances.

You can be astraddle two or more of these levels, trying to satisfy some unfinished aspects of one level while getting a toe-hold on one or more higher levels.

Fix Figure 9 firmly in mind, for it can give you great understanding of the needs and actions of family members, employees, bosses, and associates. Also mobs, organized groups, and nations.

RECOGNITION–KEY TO HUMAN RELATIONS

A practical joker once sent this telegram to ten friends: "Just heard about your latest accomplishment. Write me all about it."

Seven of the ten wrote him long letters telling about their recent achievements!

Did you ever attend a social gathering where some prominent person was present—someone you had met casually in the past? Remember how uncomfortable you were when he seemed to ignore you, how glowing you felt when he came up to you and addressed you by name? He gave you a much-desired recognition.

We all have deep-stirred cravings for attention—recognition—friendly overtures—respect—crumbs of praise. Yet we fail to give them to others, who need them as much as we do—a nod, a smile, a wave of the hand, a pat on the back.

Even the words "please" and "thank you" have recognition value: the least expensive words in the English language, if you use them; the most expensive, if you fail to use them.

Learn to be an *attention-giver* and the nicest things will happen to you. Getters don't get—givers get.

Psychologists who have studied the basic yearning for recognition have come up with four principles:

No. 1—Give recognition to a person's pretensions. Each person you meet harbors some secret feelings of excellence, of superiority —as an excellent speller, mathematician, swimmer, ice skater, dancer, card player, joke teller, singer or what have-you.

Discover these vanities, these pretensions, these hopes. Frequently they have some foundation in fact—the individual has previously been favorably cited for them, has avidly developed certain attributes or abilities, covets further recognition for them.

Flattery—an undeserved compliment—will not do. It makes the recipient feel suspicious of your motives, or perhaps feel guilty. The one who gives flattery gives nothing; the person who accepts it gets less. But a recognition of some above-average trait will draw someone toward you.

No. 2—Give praise when it is due. The accent here is on the phrase, "when it is due." Some wag has defined praise as "what a fellow gets after he's dead." Don't wait.

No. 3—Praise the work, not the worker. The person responsible for the accomplishment will understand that indirectly he, too, is being praised. If you praise the person, others may be jealous or secretly feel that you are showing favoritism. But praising outstanding results encourages others to try.

No. 4—Praise the work in front of others. Let all concerned see what you regard as good accomplishment. This practice raises the self-esteem of the doer and motivates him to repeat or redouble his efforts. In essence, it's double praise.

Setting goals and standards of performance for others becomes important, especially if these objectives have been established by discussion and mutual agreement. Then, accomplishment followed by praise is doubly motivating.

Goals should be impersonal, not merely competition with some other person.

The wise parent, for example, will not compare Tom's school work with that of older brothers Dick and Harry. If Tom is potentially smarter, he is not challenged to develop; if not as smart, he becomes frustrated, begins to hate his older brothers.

No, the wise parent will set a goal for Tom which is just a wee bit harder than anything he has ever done. When Tom accomplishes it, *the result* is praised, so motivating the boy to reach for new-set goals.

Want to prove to yourself whether recognition is really the key to better human relations? I give you a challenge:

List ten people who touch your life—wife, children, relatives, boss, subordinates, friends. Beside each name write some way you will give recognition—praise, seek out, ask for help, reach out a helping hand, offer some token of esteem, write a letter, make a phone call.

As you follow through on each one, check it off. What was the recipient's reaction? Additionally, how do *you* feel after doing all those extrovert things?

Withholding deserved praise damages human relations, can even cause tragedy. Wives complain that they are taken for granted by husband and children. Husbands secretly feel that they are unappreciated.

IF YOU BOSS OTHERS

If you are a supervisor, you soon realize the need for understanding human relations. For example, there are times when you must criticize, even though you would like to avoid it. Poorly handled, criticism may destroy the climate of confidence between you and a subordinate, may even cause a blow-up. Properly handled, it may build his loyalty.

In an interview where you must criticize, follow these practices:

1. Ask yourself honestly whether you have trained him properly.
2. Defer the interview if either you or the employee is physically tired or under emotional stress.
3. The interview should be private, away from distractions.
4. Comment on his methods or results—not on his intentions.
5. Ask questions; do not accuse or belittle.
6. If many traits need correction, select one or two simple suggestions for the first session. If you can't win with the easy points, you certainly won't with the difficult ones.
7. In offering constructive criticism, sandwich it between two points of praise or recognition.

8. Later, if the employee does better, praise the improvement.
9. If he fails to improve, at the next interview, ask him to analyze jointly with you the reasons for failure.
10. If at first you don't succeed, try, try again.

If you supervise others, or expect to some day, note this: statistical research is proving the value to a supervisor of people-orientation, a high sounding name for good human relations. You can greatly improve your supervisory ability by recognizing the value of recognition. Here are some suggestions:

1. Call each employee by name the first time you see him each day, and use his name each time you talk to him.
2. Occasionally mention to an employee his superior traits, but not in the presence of other employees.
3. Powerize your instructions, your requests, your commendations by advance selection of "trigger words." (These trigger words are discussed in the next chapter.) And smile!
4. In giving praise, observe the four principles presented earlier in the "Recognition—Key to Human Relations" section.
5. Involve employees in agreeing upon work goals and procedures.
6. Compare an employee's performance against a *standard* which you and he have jointly agreed upon—not against the production of other workers.
7. When you are receiving suggestions or complaints, listen attentively. Don't interrupt. Rephrase to prove that you have understood. Delay your decision to get more facts and to deliberate. Give your decision and the reasons for it.

For eight hours each working day, you, as a boss, are endowed with mystical powers: you hold in your hands elation or misery for those who work for you. Psychologists have given you a simple key to unlock the flood gates of happiness for your subordinates. The key is *recognition*.

True leaders in all walks of life build up their followers, make them feel important and needed. The "followers" may be part of an organized group—but they may also be friends, acquaintances, social contacts, or family members.

Virtually all the positive actions advocated in this and succeeding chapters will convert people to your views and hopes. Recipients will follow you, or at least be sympathetic and helpful to what you are trying to accomplish. Patience coupled with positive tactics can even convert dubious or hostile contacts into believers in your cause.

One important form of recognition is a consultative relationship. People believe to the extent that they participate. Their very involvement in the achievement of goals strengthens their "follower-ship."

Figure 10 may shake you up a bit, for it covers ten biting aspects of your relations to others. Very few of us, indeed, can honestly check the last right-hand column on all ten attributes. Study, for possible improvement, the items where you have rated yourself low.

FIGURE 10
Your social development

In each of the ten lines below, check the block which comes closest to your self-appraisal. If you can't decide between two blocks, check the narrow space between them. Be honest, but not harsh with yourself!

Factor	2	3	4	5	6	7	8	9	10
Attitude	I have to fight my way in this world		I have a lot of mean opposition		Some of my associates are O.K.		A few people want to help me		Most people are friendly and fair-minded
Participation	I never join in any group activity		I take part very reluctantly		Occasionally I'll take a minor role		I'm active in one or two groups		I take an active part in various groups
Communi-cation	People just don't under-stand me		They won't listen to me		I communi-cate with some but not all		I make an ef-fort to com-municate with others		I communicate well and easily with others
Empathy	People's problems are their own fault		I have enough problems of my own		I feel sorry for those less fortunate		I'll help my friends and relatives		I put myself in others' shoes and help them
Self-confidence	I have no confidence with other people		I feel un-comfortable in certain groups		Sometimes I wonder if I'm accepted		I believe people like and respect me		I'm almost always self-confident
Poise	I fall apart under pressure		I get jittery too easily		Sometimes I lose my "cool"		Mostly I'm in control of my emotions		I maintain poise even in trying situations
Adjustment	Life is unfair and cruel		It's tough, but I'm fighting on		Occasionally I'm thrown "off center"		Usually I can "roll with the blows"		I change what I can, adjust to the rest
Temperament	Folks say I have a bad temper		I have some foul moods		Sometimes I'm angry or depressed		I'm at peace with myself most of the time		I rarely get excited or dejected
Appearance	I don't bother about this		I'm afraid I'm careless		Sometimes I fail to look my best		I'm usually neat, but not fastidious		I'm careful about appear-ance and grooming
Personality	People are hostile to me		They pay little atten-tion to me		I have a few friends		I'm well accepted by many		I'm sought after

7

How well do you communicate?

In meeting people, you find yourself instantly attracted to some, indifferent to many, repelled by others.

How many times have you liked someone at the first contact, but later discovered some annoying quirks in that person? How many times have you disliked someone "instanter" who ultimately became a good friend?

Xenophobia is a word which means fear of strangers, or resentment toward them. "Strangers," in the sense here used means persons of a different race, language, religion, political persuasion, social status, or other attribute differing from you and the group to which you belong. The phobia includes fixed ideas about those other persons.

Names are important. Pronounce them properly and use them freely. If you do, you'll remember them longer. And mention your own name at the second and third contacts with new acquaintances, so saving face for them.

AFFECTIVE WAVES

Children soon come to hear disapproving dissonance in the "music" of parents' tones—or the harmony in affection shown by a word, a glance, a hug. Adults are even more finely attuned to negative and positive "vibrations" in communication, whether words are spoken or not.

Both kinds of communication generate affective waves of expansion. The foreman who had a spat with his wife at breakfast picks on a subordinate for some minor negligence. The subordinate, in turn, stewing over the boss's nagging, yells at his helper, who— and so the negative wave rolls on.

Fortunately, there are positive waves of expansion. The wife, praised for a delightful meal, is sympathetic to her husband's tribulations at work; he helps ten-year-old Johnny with his homework, and Johnny plays with five-year-old Jenny, who hugs their dog affectionately.

What kind of waves do you make?

Humility helps, as exemplified by the prayer of the government economist who prayed, "Make my words sweet, Oh Lord, for tomorrow I may have to eat them."

YOU, THE SENDER

If you take the initiative in a situation, you are the sender. If it is a two-way conversation you are also a receiver. As sender, here are some things to do, and some to avoid:

1. Know what you want to say, or what action you want to elicit. We all know how embarrassing it is to start to tell a joke, and then to forget the punch line. But it's worse if the receiver doesn't know what you're trying to put across, or what action he is expected to take.
2. Use eyeball-to-eyeball contact. The receiver subconsciously feels uncertain if you fail to look him in the eye. This principle holds true even in public speaking—if as speaker you look at as many in your audience as you can reach, you'll put your story over better than if you fix your gaze on some spot in the back of the room.
3. Avoid nose-to-nose proximity. Each receiver needs to maintain a "psychic distance" between himself and you. So don't get your face so close that you can see his tonsils; he'll feel threatened if you do.
4. Status relationships are important. Is the boss talking to an employee, or vice versa? Or is the status factor not present? The socioeconomic status of sender and receiver can affect the

communication. When a millionaire talks, people listen, even if
he's a nincompoop.
5. Gestures, posture, facial expression and tone of voice are communication devices. A friendly pat on the back says one thing;
wagging an admonishing finger, something else. A relaxed
position carries a different message than standing over the
receiver in a threatening manner. Smiles attract, frowns repel.
A loud voice arouses antagonism, whereas "a soft answer
turneth away wrath."

> At one time I was present at the regular weekly meeting of 18 fore-
> men with their plant manager. He was stressing the importance of not
> criticizing an employee in the presence of his fellow workers. Then he
> turned to one foreman and said, "That's aimed at you, Jim; you do it
> all the time."

LISTENING—A DISAPPEARING ART

Too often, we hear but do not listen. Put in another way: We
may hear the words, but not the music.

Folks will like you if you encourage them to talk about their
accomplishments, their fears, their dreams. Show respect for their
viewpoints, even though you may disagree.

Listening is at its best when the other fellow has a grievance.
Someone has defined a grievance as an idea with a stick of dyna-
mite tied to its tail. Listening may defuse it. If necessary, give a
little prompting to get complete complaint drainage.

If you're expected to make a decision or to do something about
it, summarize what the complainant has said to show that you have
understood. Usually it is desirable to delay action or decision,
perhaps saying, "Let me think about this situation. We'll talk about
it again tomorrow."

This reaction gives the complainant a chance to calm down, and
you a chance to get more information. Moreover, it gives you time
to figure out a "funnel," whereby you can point the power of his
emotions in some constructive channel—whether you accede to or
deny the request.

Sometimes we fail to listen because we don't want to listen.
Remember the bromide, "Don't confuse me with facts, I've already

made up my mind." Not infrequently, the things we don't want to hear could be more beneficial to us if we did hear them than those we listen to with eager assent.

But who wants to pay attention to those who disagree with us? We seek out people who agree with us; we read periodicals that say the things we like to hear. Too seldom do we dispassionately examine the opposing case.

Listen with an open mind, neither to embrace nor discredit. Time enough to evaluate, pro or con, after you have comprehended. And you can't comprehend if you don't listen.

THE RECEIVER

The comprehension level of the receiver enters into the equation. There's no sense in using words the receiver doesn't understand, for words are merely tags attached to ideas; unattached (not understood), the tags have no value.

The receiver may have poor health, bad eyesight, a hearing deficiency, be in the throes of an emotional upset, or lacking in intelligence. Any of these handicaps can restrict communication.

Sometimes the sender is at a lower status level than the receiver (e.g. a subordinate making verbal or written reports to the boss). If the report recommends radical changes in procedure, the sender-subordinate may encounter resistance to change. In this situation the report should: (1) promise the boss benefits he should want; (2) tell him how the proposed plan will achieve those benefits; and (3) state clearly what actions the boss should take to get the promised benefits. (This "1-2-3" formula has applicability in many human relations directions.)

THE "CLIMATE"

The conditions under which communication takes place can accelerate or impede it. "Climate" can refer to the psychological relationships existing between sender and receiver (often called the "climate of confidence"), or to the physical surroundings at the time.

If past relationships have been satisfying, progress will be made in discussing new situations. If you trust someone, or know that he has been helpful to your interests, you assume that this relationship continues.

If a third party is present, he may have an effect on the "climate." If a number of others are present, you have a group psychology which can be quite different than the interpersonal relationships between two persons.

If the environment is noisy or otherwise unpleasant, communication will be impeded. If diverting interests are present, as at a sports event, useful communication becomes difficult. No salesman would try to close a deal at a baseball game with a tie score, bases loaded, and two out in the ninth inning.

THE MESSAGE

The message is the heart of communication, whether it is written or verbal. The receiver immediately asks himself, "How does this message affect *me*?" If it controverts his aims or self-image, he will violently oppose it. If it would seem to be in his self-interest, he will embrace it. Sometimes its impact is neutral, suggesting no effect one way or the other on his life.

The message should be clear as to meaning and connote some motivation for its acceptance or execution. Clarity implies comprehension; if action is needed, the message should tell who is to do what, and when.

Where feasible, the sender should get feedback on his message: Was it understood by the receiver, and did it accomplish its purpose?

In written messages, use clear, direct statements and specific words. Suppose I rewrite the previous sentence like this: "If you are undertaking the preparation of written reports, it is desirable that you avoid the inclusion of unclear statements or make implications which are indirect in character, utilizing words which are so generalized as to fail to convey the intended meaning." Better or worse?

In this sentance their are three mispelled words. Did you spot them? Educated recipients expect good spelling. If you're unsure about some word, look it up in a dictionary before you release your written message.

GROUP LOYALTIES

Throughout our lives we join various groups—church, clubs, political party, associations, union, companies, etc. We subscribe, more or less wholeheartedly, to the aims of such groups, and participate in their activities pretty much as we believe in those aims.

Sometimes the goals of one group conflict with those of another, in which case we suffer the pangs of divided loyalties.

If you are caught in the wringer of divided loyalties, resolve it in favor of one or the other, lest you be torn asunder. You cannot long endure trying to serve two masters.

COMMUNICATIONS WITHIN GROUPS

There are some communication differences between you and another person as against you and a group to which you belong. The group expects that you will support its aims and conform to its standards of conduct. It will punish nonconformists, as mavericks soon discover.

Most voluntary associations of people elevate one member to leadership, which soon leads to some form of structured organization. Duties are delegated, and interrelationships are settled.

Communication can then be written (constitution, bylaws, organization chart, functional descriptions, agreements, etc.). Much communication is verbal, and some communication is below the verbal level—attitudes, self-interests, antagonisms, support, expectations, subconscious feelings of comfort or uneasiness.

Most organized groups become united against nonmembers and may become so imbued with self-importance that they infringe on the rights of others, or consciously conspire against them.

In addition to concurrence with group aims, members may bring various individualistic aims which they hope to satisfy through membership. The weight of these hidden objectives, seldom brought out into the open, will nevertheless be evident in discussions of group problems.

One member wants to become president of the group. One joined because he was lonely; another, for business contacts; yet another, to acquire technical information. A recent member is dedicated to the group objectives; sitting beside him is one who merely wants the prestige of belonging.

A wise leader comes to identify these hidden needs and tries to assign duties which will satisfy them, in part at least.

Consider groups to which you belong. Are you in accord with their respective aims? Do they promise to satisfy some of your hidden aspirations? If not, are there other groups which would serve you better?

COMMUNICATION IN THE HOME

Home life is society's greatest determinant of individual happiness or its opposite.

Married love can be likened to a tall ladder whose uprights are self-esteem on the one hand and regard for your partner on the other. The bottom rungs are mere sexual gratification; the two highest rungs are unselfish devotion and the ecstasy of oneness. Communication can run the gamut from hatred through malicious hurting and punishing remarks to tolerance, friendliness, palship, affection, and enthralling love.

If you are married, ask yourself what rung of this ladder you have achieved.

Communication with children, particularly teenagers, is an entirely different ballgame. Babies need cuddling, touching, bodily warmth, parental smiles and dulcet tones. Young children need assurance, discipline, security, affection, and freedom from threats. Adolescents need encouragement, challenge, assurance of parental love, respect from parents that they have become individuals in their own right.

Bear in mind the words of the humorist: It takes 14 muscles to smile but 49 muscles to frown. So conserve energy, and smile. And realize that it takes less time and energy to knock a structure down than to build it up. So be patient with your bewildered and bewildering offspring.

All these wholesome ego-sustaining influences can be conveyed to children by the many communication avenues discussed in this chapter. Neglect, harsh treatment, and deprivation of parental love almost guarantees to children neuroticism in adult life.

BECOME A WORD MASTER

Down through the centuries, leaders have recognized the motivating power of certain words. Emotion-drenched phrases have stilled mobs and thrilled nations. Consider:

"Blood, toil, tears and sweat."—Churchill

"They shall not pass."—Clemenceau

"I will return."—MacArthur

"Come unto me, all ye that . . . are heavy laden and I will give you rest."—Jesus Christ

Trigger words are power-packed messages, dripping with energizing emotion; this very sentence is an example. Contrast these two ways of saying the same things:

You look fine.	You are positively radiant.
This tire is worn and dangerous.	This tire will put your family in the hospital.
You handled a difficult situation.	You solved a problem no one had ever licked.
He's quite ordinary.	He's disgustingly uncouth.

Trigger words can be nouns, verbs, adjectives or adverbs. Here are some examples:

	Ordinary word	Trigger word
Nouns	dirt	muck
	group	horde
	liking	ardor
Verbs	walks	dashes
	wants	yearns
	says	asserts
Adjectives	dangerous	death-dealing
	pretty	radiant
	soft	velvety
Adverbs	angrily	spitefully
	soon	immediately
	well	outstandingly

In sales work, customers can sometimes be persuaded to buy if the salesman will use well-selected nouns, verbs, adjectives, and adverbs. Let's triggerize that sentence: Customer action can frequently be ignited by the pre-selected use of word-picture nouns, inciting verbs, pregnant adjectives and provocative adverbs.

Beginning to get the idea? You can have fun with it. Write out some of the ordinary things you say to your wife, children, friends, boss, fellow-workers. Introduce some ego-stirring trigger words. Powerize your compliments. Results may be dramatic, heart warming, soul stirring!

A special kind of triggerizing is the use of *pedestal words,* which raise the other fellow up on a pedestal. Here are some examples:

> I need your skilled help . . .
> I sure appreciate . . .
> Because of your specialized knowledge . . .
> You will make rapid progress.
> What is your opinion?
> You are so right.
> Spare time from your busy life . . .
> Your abilities . . .
> Based on your wide experience . . .
> As you of course know . . .
> A man of your standing . . .
> Your success . . .
> May I?
> Please . . .

Again, sheer flattery will fail. If the other fellow is not skilled or knowledgeable, he knows it. You know it. And he knows you know it. But most folks do have opinions, do believe that they lead busy lives, have had some experience, do think they have some standing. Pedestal words boost them up to a higher level of self-esteem.

Napoleon once said, "There are only two powers in the world, the sword and the pen; in the end, the former is always conquered by the latter." This, from a military genius!

In all your contacts, learn to powerize your conversation with trigger words. People's wants stir deep in their vanities, frustrations, and ambitions. Around each want is a vapor of emotion, like the unseen fumes that hover above a tank of gasoline. Touch off the fumes, and the whole tank explodes. Trigger words are merely the matches to set it off. The actual power is in the gasoline, not in the match. But if the match does not light, there is no explosion.

HOW'S YOUR SPEECH?

Have you ever strained your eardrums trying to understand some mumbling television performer? Or one who runs words together like typewritten letters with no spaces between? Or heard some interviewee say "and-uh" and "but-uh" until it drove you to the next station on the dial?

Maybe *you* exhibit some of these speech defects, and don't realize it. Here are some suggestions:

1. Using a tape recorder, record some natural conversation in which you take part, then play it back. Criticize your voice much as you may have criticized a TV performer.
2. If your speech is punctuated with "and-uhs," chase them out of your life. If the words don't flow readily, *pause* and wait for the words to come.
3. If your voice is unclear or slurred compared with others in the conversation, practice saying the same words, but rounding out the finals—not sing'n', but sing*ing*; not househol', but househol*d*, not carp'd, but carp*et*.
4. If you talk too fast, pause wherever you'd insert a comma or period if you were writing it.
5. If your voice is shrill or nasal, practice speaking in a lower register.
6. Watch out for senseless phrases like "Y'know what I mean" or "See?"
7. Clean up your speech, much as you'd clean up a cluttered attic in your home.
8. Avoid double and triple negatives. For example, "don't avoid the lack of disinterest." (Who knows what it means?)
9. Avoid ambiguous meanings. For example, "She was washing a French poodle in a fur coat, shivering all the while."
10. Use specific words, rather than generalized. Say "young girl," rather than "female"; "accountant," rather than "employee"; "Cadillac," rather than "vehicle." Paint word pictures, and you'll become a word artist.

FIVE KINDS OF COMMUNICATION

Figure 11 illustrates five kinds of communication: Note the four symbols at the top of the figure:

A. One-way communication, as when a parent commands a child, or a boss gives a direct order to a subordinate.

B. Two-way, in which there is either a back-and-forth discussion, or a feedback to the original sender.

C. A casual discussion group, largely dominated by two senders. Note that one individual, shown by the lone circle, receives but sends nothing (i.e., contributes nothing to the discussion).

D. Autocratic group leadership, in which the big boss tells 'em, and they carry out his orders.

E. Consultative group leadership, in which there is free interchange between the leader and his followers, and among the followers.

Various combinations of these five types are possible.

If you are leading a group, here's a procedure which will win the respect of group members:

1. Use a blackboard (or large tablet with crayon).
2. Write at the top of the blackboard the objective of the meeting.
3. Bring up important questions. If no one volunteers ideas, call upon qualified members to offer suggestions.
4. Record *pertinent* ideas on the blackboard.
5. Classify ideas under logical subheadings. Useful subheadings are contained in Rudyard Kipling's quatrain:

> I kept six faithful serving men—
> They taught me all I knew
> Their names are what and how and when,
> And why and where and who.

6. By this time, the answer to the posed problem, or a course of procedure, should be obvious to the group. Get a member to state it explicitly and record it on the blackboard.
7. It is good practice to send a written report of conclusions to all participants, and include a deadline for action or completion.

FIGURE 11
Five kinds of communication

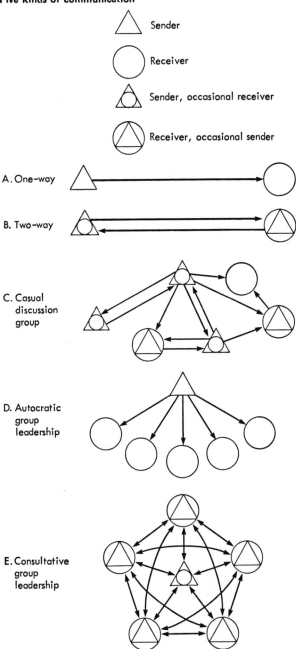

8. Prior to the deadline, send a reminder to those responsible for execution.
9. At the deadline, appraise actual performance.
10. Praise good performance (but not the performer) before other members of the group.

Leadership is more than exhortation. Following the ten steps above will transform a leader into an administrator.

Harsh words can prevent or destroy communication, for they echo back on both parties like the sound of stones dropped into a deep well. Just as positive power words can trigger happy emotions, so negative words can stir anger or other negative reactions. Criticism, sarcasm, punishing remarks, or odious comparisons etch deep, cutting ego channels through which resentment quickly flows.

Finally, in your conversation dwell neither on your merits nor your weaknesses. Your friends have already noted the former, your enemies the latter.

BE PREPARED

Many events in your life can be planned in advance. The salesman gets information on his prospect's business and special interests before the interview. He asks himself what objections are likely to be raised, and prepares the answers. He practices any physical demonstration so it will come off smoothly.

You are a salesman of yourself in every human encounter. You, too, can frequently get advance information, can practice what you expect to say and do.

A friend of mine is known as a brilliant conversationalist, and gets invited to many and varied evening groups. When I asked him his secret, he replied, "It's no secret at all. I find out the interests of people who will be present and read up on those subjects. This knowledge permits me to ask intelligent questions, which they are delighted to answer. Moreover, this practice continually adds to my own store of knowledge."

If you will candidly analyze how well you communicate with others, taking into account the many suggestions in this chapter, you will be known as a brilliant conversationalist and be elected to high office in many endeavors.

It's true. I dare you to try to prove me wrong.

COMMUNICATION FAILURES

Failure of sender and receiver to communicate on the same wave length causes much of the misery and misunderstanding between two people, groups or nations. Conversation between just two acquaintances can often supply examples of communication failure, where a common ground of understanding is lacking. Sometimes, one or the other is bored. The humorist defines a bore as "one who wants to talk when I want to talk." Such individuals monotonize the conversation.

Man's wisdom has some pithy comments on such a situation: You never learn anything, talking. The Good Lord gave you two ears, but only one tongue. Your ears should get more exercise than your tongue. They always talk who never think. Those who think in inches, but talk by the yard, should be given the foot. Utter the word "You" ten times as much as "I."

Finally, to be a delightful conversationalist, you need occasional flashes of silence.

8
Your body–Source of power

Your health and energy are inextricably tied in with your happiness and success. Hence, the more you understand about your body and how it functions, the more likely your satisfying progress.

Most of us take our bodies for granted—until something goes wrong. Then we expect a physician to give us some miracle drug to get rid of whatever ails us. However, as pointed out in previous chapters, improper diet, lack of exercise, or bad living habits may have so undermined a certain organ that drugs prove of no avail. It may be necessary to strengthen the "whole man," both mind and body, not just the weak-link organ which first signals that something is wrong.

YOUR BODY

The human body is a marvelous organism. You can learn to use it intelligently for your own advancement and success. It consists of living cells, differentiated as to purpose, and organized into a bony skeleton, outer skin, various (special-purpose) organs (such as heart, lungs, stomach, kidneys, liver, spleen, gall bladder and intestines), a circulatory system, a nervous system (which includes the brain), and small but powerful ductless glands. This list is not complete.

In this book, we are mainly interested in the nervous system and the ductless glands—and how they affect your development and success. In this chapter we will discuss the nervous system. Ductless glands will be discussed in later chapters.

YOUR NERVOUS SYSTEM

Your brain is the seat of thought; all nerve routes run to and from it. It observes your environment, evaluates it and commands fight, flight, inaction, creativity, or some other response.

The brain consists of (1) the cerebrum (thinking), (2) the cerebellum (body coordination), and (3) medulla oblongata and brainstem (the mid-brain which connects brain and spinal cord).

The interrelationships among the brain parts, including as they do an estimated 12 *billion* nerve cells, boggle the imagination—not to mention their other nerve relationships to all parts of the body. Comparable, might be one central switchboard which connected every telephone on earth!

The spinal cord is a kind of cable connecting the brain and most nerves of the voluntary nervous system (save for 12 pairs of nerves in the head). It is protected by the bones (vertebrae) of the spinal column.

Thirty-one pairs of spinal nerves emerge between the vertebrae. Sensory (afferent) nerves bring impulses (sensations) to the spinal cord; motor (efferent) nerves carry directions outward to muscles and organs. If the brain need not be involved (as in reacting to a pinprick), the situation is known as a "reflex," or "reflexive action." The brain may know about it (pain) after the action, but many reflex actions occur at nonthinking levels.

As already indicated, nerves carry messages to and from processing centers, such as the brain and spinal cord. A nerve (neuron) is a living cell which has "receiving antennae" (dendrites) and transmitting "wires" (axons). If a nerve *cell* is destroyed, it is gone forever.

Your body contains billions of neurons, associated together in an almost incomprehensible maze. Fortunately, nerves do not tire or wear out with use—but they can be destroyed by disease or accident, or impaired by malnutrition.

THE SYMPATHETIC NERVOUS SYSTEM

The term "sympathetic" is a misnomer; involuntary (auto-nomic) is a better term. Situated outside, but close to the voluntary nervous system, it regulates automatic activities such as blood circulation, heartbeat, breathing, digestion, peristaltic action of intestines, and so forth. In emergency situations, this system arouses the resisting forces of the body in a few seconds.

The involuntary system is more primitive than the voluntary; eons ago it was necessary for survival of the forerunners of man. It functions in animals much the same as in man; that is, it adapts to the environment, and prepares the body for fight or flight when indicated.

We have little direct control of the involuntary nervous system, but our positive or negative moods can repress or stimulate bodily functions. Thus, when you're sad, you don't want to eat; frightened, your heart will beat faster; embarrassed, your cheeks may flush.

Just as there are contracting (agonist) and opposing (antagonist) muscles in your body, so there are activating (sympathetic) and opposing (parasympathetic) nerves in the involuntary system.

When mind and body are in harmony, we feel a sense of well-being. When either one or the other is out of whack, there is un-balance; you may say, "I feel terrible." If you continue feeling terrible long enough, you may end up with high blood pressure or a gastric ulcer.

THE WINDOWS OF YOUR MIND

Most of your knowledge comes to you through your five senses: sight, hearing, smell, taste and touch. Some authorities assert that we possess other senses—a "sixth" sense (intuition); a muscle sense (heft or perception of weight); pain, imagination, and others.

Sensory organs (eyes, ears, etc.) can be trained to high degrees of sensory acuity. On the other hand, their powers can be lessened, or completely lost, through neglect or the aging process. Aging is irreversible, but it can be slowed by proper diet and living habits, such as suggested in previous chapters. These habits include good hygiene for the eyes and ears, the two senses which are most susceptible to deterioration. Their care in the young and middle years will pay off in the later years, when all your physical powers are on the wane.

BODY REACTIONS

Your body has a number of ways by which it sustains life or reacts to its environment. Automatic responses are one. These are hereditary and mediated largely through the autonomic (involuntary) nervous system.

Reflexes are also hereditary, but are mediated largely through the spinal cord. A definite stimulus elicits a definite response. Examples are recoiling from a hot stove, closing eyelids against a flying object, starting at a loud noise, sneezing.

Reflexes can be "conditioned" as exemplified by Pavlov's famous experiment. A bell was sounded each time a dog was to be given meat; the animal's reaction to sight of the meat was a flow of saliva. After a time the sound of the bell alone would cause the dog's mouth to water—a conditioned reflex. When you brake your automobile at the sight of a red traffic light, you are obeying a conditioned reflex.

Habits are a third way we adapt to our environment. All habits are learned, usually (but not necessarily) through trial and error, and may ultimately become extremely complex. Habits are great time savers. At the beginning stage of learning a new habit, mental effort is required but as the habit becomes well-established, consciousness tends to drop out. Driving an automobile provides an excellent example.

There are four principal kinds of habit formation: (1) muscular, (2) mental, (3) social, and (4) emotional. By the time you are an adult, you have built hundreds of habits. Most are so ingrained that you no longer are aware of them.

Most manual skills embrace observation and sensory—motor (i.e., muscular)—coordinations. Riding a bicycle provides a simple example; playing a pipe organ, a complex example.

Mental habits include observation, reasoning, and attitudes. Exemplifying observation habits, consider what a botanist and a geologist would each "see" on a mountain hike. As to reasoning, some individuals jump to hasty conclusions, whereas others withhold a conclusion until they have scrutinized all available facts. Attitudes are mental sets—habitual ways of considering various situations.

Social habits depend on the mores (customs) of the group to which you belong. These traditional practices change slowly from one generation to another. Consider dancing in the 18th-century French Court, in the 19th-century U.S. frontier towns, and at a 20th-century "rock" festival.

Much real progress in your life depends on building good habits. William James, recognized as both philosopher and psychologist, once wrote, "Sow an action and you reap a habit; sow a habit and you reap a character; sow a character and you reap a destiny."

Not only are good habits time and energy savers, but they avoid inertia in initiating action and help you get a lot of things done well and in good time (and thus are called "skills").

Even success or failure can become habitual. Thrice defeated, hope departs; thrice a winner, success assured. This principle is particularly important in assigning difficult, but achievable tasks to children so that they will build the habit of success.

INSTINCTS

Instincts, or drives, are terms that are subjects of dispute among psychologists. Newborn fish swim, birds soon learn to fly; salmon swim upstream to lay their eggs; most animals take care of their young; lions kill other animals only when they're hungry. These actions are classed as instincts; they are innate behavior that does not have to be learned, quite complex but subject to some modification.

Mankind undoubtedly possesses some innate drives, and these have been variously classified by different psychologists. In a complex civilization, these drives manifest themselves in many guises. Here's a classification which I have found helpful:

1. Dominance—Assertiveness, competitiveness, persistence, display, desire for power, leadership, mastery, fighting, struggles for freedom, curiosity, exploration.
2. Submission—Acceptance, following, self-abasement, religiousness.
3. Creativeness—Designing, constructing, repairing, manipulating,

original research, creative writing, artistic expression, solution of puzzles.

4. Possessiveness—The fun of acquiring; the joy of owning; the enjoyment of collecting and classifying; protection of property.
5. Gregariousness—Desire to be part of a group; desire to get (sometimes give) sympathy or social approval; joining; teamwork; or spirit.
6. Homing—Sex, love and mating; parental protectiveness; homemaking to provide food, shelter, and security.

These basic drives assert themselves in different individuals in different ways at different times. Hence, understanding human behavior (including your own inconsistencies) becomes a complex, withal fascinating, subject.

> The college football hero (dominant) may listen respectfully in the mathematics class (submission); enjoy a course in art (creativeness); collect foreign coins (possessiveness); crave admission to a fraternity (gregariousness); and be engaged to the girl of his choice (homing). Yet 30 years later, these same drives may appear in different forms, and with different intensities.

The powerful feelings associated with one of these drives in human beings is known as an "emotion." An emotion is the consciousness of numerous bodily changes resulting from stress of some sort. These changes are initiated by hormones acting on heart, lungs, liver, digestion, sweat glands, and blood circulation. We shall consider emotions in later chapters, for they are the source of your greatest happiness—and unhappiness.

SITUATION—BOND—RESPONSE

Much human behavior conforms to a single pattern: situation, bond, response. Let us consider some examples:

Reflex. You touch a hot object. Your involuntary nervous system directs your muscles to withdraw quickly.

Habit. Your alarm clock goes off. It is time to get up. You dress.

Habit. You sneeze (a reflex). Some total stranger says, "God bless you."

Instinct. One peaceful Sunday morning, unable to find a parking place, you drive into the parking lot of a closed food store. A passerby yells, "You can't park there," but you do so nevertheless. He threatens, "I'll smash your teeth in." You get out of your car and say, "Let's see you try it." He walks away, muttering to himself.

In this last instance, situation, bond (your anger), and response (your action) are simple and almost instantaneous. Sometimes, one or all three are prolonged, as in the following:

> A young, timid student was drafted into the army. In barracks a bully delighted in harassing him—dumping his cot, pulling off his blankets, and so forth. Finally, the young man can take it no longer; he forces the bully into a shallow closet and locks him in, standing, for three hours. That ends the bullying. Fifteen years later, the one-time student has his own business and the one-time bully applies to him for a job. He doesn't get it.

In this case the situation (bullying) was prolonged; the bond (resolve to fight back) was delayed; there was one delayed response (the closet), but another delayed response 15 years later (the rejection for a job).

Sometimes you can predict a response when you know the situation. However, it is not so easy, given some dramatic response, to determine the situations and the bonds (thought) which brought about the response. A case in point would be a seemingly happy married couple who announce to their friends that they plan to divorce.

ENEMIES OF YOUR BODY

Your body is constantly at war with enemies that would destroy it, principally bacteria and viruses. There are, however, other enemies: physical trauma (accidents); extreme heat or cold; deprivation of food, water, or affection; chemicals (poisons for example); environment (such as air and water pollution); wild animals; human enemies; last but not least, your own emotions.

Considering all that the human body must contend with, it's a wonder that mankind has survived to this day. Your body must indeed be both adaptable and resistant.

Bacteria (germs) have been identified for almost a century,

beginning with the pioneer work of a French scientist, Louis Pasteur. Since that time, numerous germ-killing drugs have appeared, such as sulfa (sulphonamides) and penicillin. Some wag has remarked that we have so many new drugs that we don't as yet have diseases for them.

So far no effective drugs have been developed against viruses. These are so tiny that 60 thousand would measure about 1/16 of an inch. They are not living creatures like germs, but are chemical substances which can multiply themselves very rapidly. Fortunately, the body builds its own immunity to most viral diseases, such as the "flu," the common cold, or smallpox.

Negative emotions, long sustained, can reduce the ability of your body to resist or to overcome bacterial and viral infections. Unhappy people are likely to be unhealthy people, as we shall discuss in Chapter 12.

CHARACTER ANALYSES MYTHS

Anthropologists have studied various structural shapes of human beings, classifying them roughly as endomorphs—protruding abdomens; ectomorphs—lean and slightly muscular; and mesomorphs—powerful musculature and bony framework.

Anthropologists have discovered some tendencies for these three types to vary in mental and emotional attributes, but not with sufficient certainty that the structural signs can be used in current judgments or predictions as to the future. The caution of these scientists does not deter various "character analysts" from making outrageous (but unsupported) claims for their various systems of judging people by exterior signs.

Over many centuries, man has tried to evaluate his fellows by outward signs. A large head meant high intelligence; small ears, selfishness; receding chin, timidity; small eyes, cunning, and so forth. Character analyses systems were built around some of these assumptions. Phrenology was one such; its devotees claimed that they could tell whether a person was a businessman, a musician or a murderer merely by feeling the "bumps" on his head.

Today, phrenology, craniology, and physiognomy are discredited beliefs, along with palmistry, astrology, crystal gazing, and fortune telling.

Anthropology is the making of scientific observations of man's body and physical equipment, and how they affect his progress. Physiology, biology, genetics, chemistry, and physics are fused in medical science. Psychology and sociology contribute to our knowledge of man as an individual and in groups. You will do well to follow the findings of scientists rather than glib systems or the promotions of self-serving men.

MEMORY

In a sense, you remember with your whole nervous system. There are no brain pigeonholes into which memories are filed. The sensory nerves which have received certain impressions tend to retain those impressions for later use. Thus, you can recall the haunting smile of a Mona Lisa painting, the sound of your mother's voice, the aroma of fresh coffee, the taste of a lemon, the touch of velvet, the cold of ice, the burn from a match, the weight of a two-pound bag of sugar. Memories, all.

Suppose you had to start each day with no memories of the things you had experienced previously. With no accumulated memories, each day would be a cautious repetition of each previous day. You would build no habits, make no progress; the human race would soon expire.

Memory, then, can be considered a record of your past experiences. If you have memories for many things, you have progressed in many things. Some will be ideational—words, names, abstract concepts, attitudes, and integrated bodies of knowledge, such as chemistry. Some are sensory memories, mentioned above. Some may be motor (muscular coordination) memories, as in driving an automobile. You may even be able to recreate in memory past imaginative fantasies of things which never actually happened or existed.

You can sing a tune, but I bet you can't describe how you do it. Auditory (hearing) memory teams up with your vocal chords in some mysterious fashion.

Since no new nerves develop in your body after birth, memory improvement is largely a problem of interrelating (associating or integrating) existing nerve paths so that more "connections" can exist, or that by repetition present connections will be etched more deeply. The person who develops a large memory or great skills is one who carries this integration process further than his fellows.

James M. Barrie, British author, once wrote "God gave us our memories so that we might have roses in December."

Since memory underlies much that you do in life, we shall devote an entire chapter (Chapter 10) to it.

This present chapter provides a background for our consideration of various mental abilities, skills, and imagination. 'Tis said that instinct leaps, but reason crawls. In a primitive society, man had to obey his instincts. In our highly organized civilization, reason is the better master.

9

How to develop your brain power

It was Peter Drucker, author of many books on management, who early pointed out that a new class of worker had developed— the knowledge worker. The knowledge worker was neither blue-collar nor white-collar; rather, his contribution lay in his technical knowledge and skill, exemplified by a computer programmer. Or, he might be an engineer, a research scientist, a tape control specialist in a machine shop, a service mechanic for an electronic computer.

Technical information is the common denominator of knowledge workers. And such information is principally acquired through formal instruction, which steadily contributes to the upward mobility of the technically trained.

Burgeoning technology has already transformed education and will have an even greater effect in the decades ahead. In the second quarter of this century, our schools turned out students with a smattering of knowledge in arts, sciences, mathematics, English, languages. The third quarter of this century witnessed an unorganized rebellion of students against this production line type of education. Educational reform has moved in two directions:

1. Individualistic development of students, especially in the lower grades: study freedom, laxity of discipline, lowering of educational standards.

2. More specific career preparation (specialization), often at the two-year junior college level—a trend augmented by technological

developments in many areas of human knowledge, and the need for technical assistants in science, industry and service occupations. Leaders in these areas came to realize that knowledge, per se, is static but that application is dynamic.

The first direction has resulted in a deterioration of public school education, and to high school graduates who haven't even mastered the three Rs. Scores in the nationally accepted Scholastic Aptitude Test have been falling almost 1 percent each year while the cost of education has risen about 10 percent each year. For you, the implication is clear: as you acquire more education, like a champion long-distance runner, you steadily draw away from the faltering pack.

LIFE-LONG LEARNING

Our ancestors typically followed one career for a lifetime. Our parents in the current century may have had a number of jobs in different lines of work.

Continuing acceleration of technological information suggests that change will probably speed up. Hence, you should undertake life-long training. Keep alert to new developments, read books and technical magazines in several fields of interest, take advantage of courses in your community. Stand up to the future, don't let it wash over you. Heed the adage: None so ignorant as those who know not, and know not that they know not.

Experience, they say, is a great teacher—but knowledge provides a shortcut which avoids wasteful trial and error. A good general education may not suffice. Will Rogers once cracked, "No one is as stupid as an educated man when he gets into a thing he was not educated in." The acquisition of specialized knowledge is not subject to the law of diminishing returns—rather it is cumulative, like compound interest.

MORE EDUCATION

In most communities, there are "free" or low cost courses available. Many are down-to-earth, and most are taught by experienced specialists in their respective fields. (If you are unable to uncover what you need in your area, write to NEXUS, c/o American Association for Higher Education, One Dupont Circle, Suite 780, Washington, D.C. 20036.)

If you have the stamina to stay with a correspondence course, study ads which appear in various magazines devoted to the subject of your interest, such as auto mechanics, air conditioning, accounting, salesmanship. Consult your local library. If you're going to aim high, first get lots of ammunition.

You will need life-long learning if you would keep up with changing times, so find out where you can acquire added knowledge and skill of value to your career. Moving a mountain isn't too much to tackle if you take it a shovelful at a time.

As you read this book, develop your own training prescription, laying stress on things you need to know, or do, or be. You are a unique personality; no one else is like you. Find and improve your areas of weakness and you will discover that your strengths grow even stronger.

The difference for you in being excellent or just good enough may not seem to be much—but the cumulative effect of excellence in play after play in your life can spell the difference between winning, and just coming close. For the more you do to learn, the more you learn to do.

Many a wondering father has observed that his 14-year-old son possesses a greater fund of information than either parent. This situation is but one manifestation of the *knowledge explosion* of recent decades, which is surfacing in business, science, education, and the communication media.

In the business world, the "information elite" are making significant contributions to management, production and the distribution of goods and services. The sciences, too, are a cornucopia of fundamental findings which contribute to mankind's well-being—but could be the source of his ultimate destruction. Curiosity is one of man's yearnings that is seldom completely satisfied.

MENTAL ABILITIES

It is not easy to subdivide your mental abilities into neat, separate compartments, because they are intertwined. In this and succeeding chapters, we shall consider the following six, each briefly defined below:

1. *Comprehension.* Interpretation of sensory observations or of idea relationships.
2. *Memory.* Ability to recognize or recall information, events, dates, data, faces, names or ideational concepts, when needed. Chapter 10 will cover this important ability, which underlies all other mental capacities.
3. *Vocabulary.* Understanding the meaning of words read or heard, and how to use them correctly.
4. *Reasoning.* The ability to reach a correct, logical conclusion (induction) from facts presented; or to infer by applying an accepted generalization or principle to a specific situation (deduction).
5. *Space perception.* Ability to visualize in two- or three-dimensional spatial relationships, form, and color.
6. *Imagination.* The recombining of memories into new relationships and patterns; inventiveness; creativity. This subject is so important to your success that we shall devote an entire chapter to it—Chapter 11.

In seeking to solve a complex problem, you may use some or all these mental powers. A word of caution: Before you seek an answer, ask whether you have posed the right question. For instance, your self-questioning, "Should I seek another job?" might more properly be, "Have I done all I should in my present job?"

Seek the help of knowledgeable people. Only the perpetually ignorant refuse to ask questions.

Your value in a given subject or skill is shown, not so much by high specialization, as by the supporting knowledge and experience you can bring to bear on that specialization. It helps to be as versatile as a mother of six young children on a rainy day.

COMPREHENSION

Comprehension involves simple understanding but may call upon complex intuition. A child sent to the grocery store by his mother must understand her instructions before he can remember them. A student who fails to understand the meaning of a principle will not be able to apply it. A workman given instructions for possible alternative actions must understand their similarities and differences before he can decide which one to use.

On the intuitive level, if you meet some once-prosperous friend and note that his clothes are threadbare, you comprehend that he's not making out so well as in the past, despite his brave front.

Both simple understanding and complex intuition are dependent upon accurate and adequate observation. Hence, you will do well to keep an open mind toward new ideas or acquaintances, to be certain that you really understand what you see or hear and to get repeated observations before you pass your intuitive judgment. Bear in mind that you may be bringing to bear on a situation your own bias. The ancient wisdom of the Talmud declares, "We do not see things as they are; we see things as *we* are."

Those who are slow to comprehend may be dull-witted or gullible. Per contra, those who make snap judgments may be impulsive or superficial. Strive for the happy medium.

VOCABULARY

My friend Bert is the pride of his family and friends. His conversation sparkles and his letters radiate. Why? Because Bert has an unusually wide vocabulary. He is always on the lookout for new words to improve his conversational ability.

Increasing your vocabulary will not only make you more interesting and impressive, but will also markedly enhance your chances of social or business success. A good vocabulary is one earmark of a smart businessman or of an outstanding social leader.

Words are the labels of ideas. Fugitive ideas which you are unable to express in words are of little use to you. Small vocabularies mean limited mental concepts and restrict your ability to convey ideas and meanings to others, unless assisted by pictures, gestures, sounds, and signs.

Learning new words results in acquiring new meanings, providing more material for your thought processes. Most of us have a larger understanding vocabulary than we use; often context clarifies meanings of vaguely understood words. Therefore, if you are the possessor of a wide vocabulary, you can carefully choose exact words to convey specific meanings. Likewise in conversation and reading, you will be able to understand persons of high intellectual talents.

Sometimes words actually hide meanings rather than convey them. If I say to you, "Paucity of vocabulary is not infrequently unmixed blessing," do I mean it's a good thing to have a small vocabulary—or just the opposite? Learn to make direct statements unencumbered by double negatives or numerous ifs, ands and buts.

SIMPLE WAYS TO STRENGTHEN YOUR VOCABULARY

Strengthening your vocabulary means: (1) adding new words, with full understanding of their meanings; and (2) converting presently known words from existing to higher levels of usefulness.

Here are some thoughts on adding new words:

1. Get and use a good dictionary, preferably one with copious illustrations.
2. Purchase an A to Z notebook, one small enough to be carried in your pocket or handbag. Each time you encounter a new or vaguely understood word, write it in your book, even if you have to guess at the spelling.
3. Look up the meaning and correct spelling in your dictionary and record them in your notebook. In otherwise idle moments, review these new words. Consider sentences in which they might be used without "showing off." Use them in conversation and writing.
4. Do crossword puzzles, dictionary at your elbow; enter new words in your notebook.

You can convert known and new words to higher usage levels by:

1. Studying the vowel and consonant instructions, as well as accents, in your dictionary to insure correct pronunciation. Practice aloud.
2. In looking up a new word, read synonyms, derivations, variations, and other explanatory material.
3. Read aloud well-written prose and fiction. Enunciate clearly, especially with the final consonant sounds.

You do not own words which you merely read and hear; to make them yours you must use them appropriately in your speech and writing—and without pretension.

REASONING

The ability to reason distinguishes man from animals. How well you reason may distinguish you from unsuccessful people. Reasoning is the capstone of your intellect, bending other traits to its needs.

Reasoning may be brought into play by the challenge of new situations, by the necessity to choose between alternatives, by questioning accepted ideas, or by deliberate striving for new knowledge. It is dynamic, persistent, and coherent.

Leaders reason, followers accept. Logical conclusions, based on sufficient data are likely to be action-provoking. Hasty conclusions, based on insufficient or biased data can cause chaos.

A man of good judgment in one situation may reason poorly in others. I know a plant manager who carefully gathers pertinent data before making manufacturing decisions. Yet in his handling of personnel problems he relies on his hunches and fixed beliefs. He considers himself a natural handler of men—but 450 employees secretly disagree.

Reasoning is so important to your success that we shall now consider how you can greatly enhance this valuable attribute.

HOW TO IMPROVE YOUR REASONING POWERS

We have previously mentioned two kinds of reasoning: (1) Inductive—reaching a conclusion from collected data. It is synthetic, for it builds from details to principles or conclusions. (2) Deductive—applying a known conclusion or principle to a specific situation. Here are two examples: "A listing of this merchant's assets and liabilities shows that he is bankrupt" (inductive process). "Since he is bankrupt, he will not be able to pay in full his obligation to me" (deductive process).

You can improve your powers of reasoning by following five steps:

1. *Define the problem.* Make it as *specific* as you can, even if you have to express it as several specific problems. Recall that a problem clearly stated is already partially solved. For example, not "How can we improve our product line?" which is too

general, but "Should we add toothpaste to our present line of food products?"

2. *Gather pertinent data.* What information bears upon the problem; how and where do I find it? For example: We need information about toothpaste competition in our territory; our store outlets which do and do not stock toothpaste; costs of manufacturing toothpaste, advertising, and so forth.

3. *Formulate a conclusion,* after classifying data and discarding irrelevant data. For example: We discard government figures as too old and too general. We classify the remainder by marketing centers; by chain, department, drug and neighborhood grocery stores. Considering volume, profit margins, distribution problems and advertising costs, only department stores seem feasible because of high volume and low selling expense.

4. *Test the tentative conclusion* against reality. For example: By pilot plant production we stock representative small and large department stores and analyze results over a six-month period.

5. *Accept, reject or modify* the conclusion, based on experience. For example: Large department store sales are low and yield a low profit margin; small department stores show excellent gross profit. So the answer to our problem is, yes, we should add toothpaste to our product line, but concentrate on sales to small and medium-sized department stores.

For use in trying to solve problems in your life, remember these five steps:

1. Define the problem in specific terms.
2. Gather and analyze adequate, pertinent data.
3. Formulate a tentative conclusion.
4. Test the tentative conclusion.
5. Accept, reject, or modify the conclusion.

Further, realize that sometimes you can: (1) predict effects from known causes; (2) guess causes from known effects; (3) consider whether two observed events are cause and effect, or both are the result of some remote cause. Thus can we say that bad housing causes crime or that both are results of inadequate education?

In reasoning out a problem you may have to shuttle back and

forth between induction and deduction, between cause and effect or effect and cause.

SPACE PERCEPTION

Space perception (visualization) is a little recognized ability which does, however, enter into much of your daily life. It is your capacity to grasp or estimate distances, dimensions, shapes, rates of speed, or color—and their interrelationships. It is a trait needed by interior decorators, design draftsmen, surgeons, dentists, toolmakers, artists, sculptors, window dressers, and hundreds of other occupations. You use it when you pass a car on the road against oncoming traffic or when you buy a necktie to go with a colored shirt.

Here are some simple tests which will make the concept of space perception clearer to you:

1. Draw on a piece of paper what the capital letters *F* and *R* will look like if held in front of a mirror.
2. Visualize a clock which shows 26 minutes after two. If the hands are reversed approximately what time will it be?
3. Suppose you assemble 27 children's blocks into a cube 3 blocks x 3 blocks x 3 blocks. If you painted the outside of the assembled cube, how many blocks would show paint on one face only?
4. What word on this page would just about be covered by a dime?

IMPROVING YOUR SPACE PERCEPTION

You can improve your ability to visualize in the second and third dimension as well as in other aspects of space perception. Sharpening of this mental ability is accomplished by: (1) careful observation; (2) estimating; and (3) checking estimates against actuality.

Driving along an open road, I judge that a billboard is one mile away, my odometer tells me it is eight-tenths of a mile. I judge that I'm driving at 50 miles an hour, but the speedometer (or the state patrolman) says 60.

Certain shades of red and blue go well together, others clash. By putting them side by side, I improve the acuity of my color sense.

Sensory training is specific. The cutter in a clothing manufacturing plant may not be able to carry his space perception over to laying carpet. The secretary who types a neat appearing letter may botch a large tabulation of statistical data. It behooves you to study the space perceptions required in your daily life, form your own estimates, and check your estimates to improve the ability to visualize.

IMPROVE YOUR READING SPEED

Slow learners are often merely slow readers. If you laboriously read word for word, mentally saying each one, you're probably a slow reader. You can learn to read faster, and absorb more of what you cover. It's not difficult. However, as in eating, you must digest it to get the full benefit.

When you read merely for diversion, you can skim the words for meaning. Speed reading for improvement is an extension of this approach. However, when reading information which you want to retain, here are some ideas which can help:

1. Read the table of contents of a technical book to comprehend its scope; or note the subheadings of a smaller publication.
2. Pay particular attention to the opening and closing paragraphs of each chapter.
3. The first sentence of many paragraphs states what the paragraph will cover.
4. Read rapidly, scanning phrases and clauses for meaning. If you fail to catch the meaning, read again.
5. If you own the publication you are reading, underline phrases or sentences which strike you as significant.
6. If you are trying to master (i.e., remember in considerable detail) a subject, outline it with headings and subheadings on separate paper. Review your outline from time to time. This practice is of course more than mere reading—it's study.

COLLEGE, EVERYONE?

A prominent educator once said, "No one can hope for success these days unless he has a college education." Is that so, Mr.

Educator? Try telling that to the hordes of college graduates who can't get jobs in their chosen fields. Or can't get jobs—period. Or to the millions of successful salesmen, actors, writers, athletes, skilled artisans or business executives who never entered the hallowed halls of some university.

Or, recall Thomas Edison—at the bottom of his class; Henry Ford, whose teacher once wrote, "shows no promise"; Abraham Lincoln, who became a lawyer and was elected to the highest office in the land; Albert Einstein, considered "mentally slow" by his teachers. History records scores of others who made good without benefit of a college education.

The U.S. Bureau of Labor Statistics estimates that in the decade ahead the nation's institutions of higher learning will grant diplomas to almost 16 million graduates who will be competing for 15 million "college level" jobs.

In this dilemma, should you strive for a college degree—or forget it? Here are some facts to consider:

1. A college education increases your chance of *financial* success—but does not guarantee it. The U.S. Census Bureau presents these lifetime earnings figures: elementary school graduate, $192,000; high school graduate, $264,000; college graduate, $388,000; post-graduate study, $443,000.
2. Whatever your definition of success may be, a surprisingly large percentage of people achieve it without a college education. Perhaps this result is connoted in a Report of the President's Commission on Higher Education, which notes that, "at least as many young people who have the same or greater intellectual ability than those in college do not enroll because of low family income." The college degree has lost some of its allure; not having it, some of its derogation.
3. Additional learning, however gotten, is desirable in this automation age; it does not have to be obtained in a classroom.
4. The rounded development of your personal traits is more important than additional education. If this statement were not so, only highly educated people would be on all the top rungs of success.

In summary, your learning should be life-long, should include cultural development, and should be accompanied by continuing growth of personal traits. (See Figure 12 to evaluate yourself on the development of your mind.)

FIGURE 12
Have you developed your mind?

In each of the ten lines below, check the block which comes closest to your self-appraisal. If you can't decide between two blocks, check the narrow space between them. Be honest, but not harsh with yourself.

Factor	2	3	4	5	6	7	8	9	10
Education	Elementary schooling		Some high school		High school graduate		Some college or equivalent		College graduate or more
Vocabulary	Is very limited		I use simple words only		I'm about average, I think		My vocabulary is larger than average		I command a large vocabulary
Mathematics	Addition, counting, weighing		I can do multiplication and division		I can do decimals and fractions		I can use calculating machines		I use advanced complex mathematics
Limitations of tradition	I follow custom and tradition		I guess I'm really a conformist		I doubt some rules and social practices		I evaluate many traditional practices		I think things through for myself
Conversation	I rarely talk when in a group		I find it difficult to hold a conversation		I like to chat with friends		I can hold my own with strangers		I'm known as a brilliant conversationalist
Reasoning	I don't try to think things through		I jump at hasty conclusions		I want easy answers to difficult problems		I study the pros and cons		I weigh facts and test my conclusions
Music	No musical talent		I enjoy listening to music		I dabble at some musical instrument		I can play a musical instrument		I perform before audiences
Artistic sense	Art is distasteful to me		I have little artistic interest		I have some minor talent		Well-developed esthetic sense		I create something artistic
Imagination	I deal with tangible things only		I'm practical —indulge in no flights of fancy		I have an active imagination		I frequently come up with new ideas		I do novel conceptual thinking
Interests	No special interests		Mechanical matters		My job, family, and sports		Science, economics, civic affairs		Mankind, religion, philosophy

10
How to improve your memory

You have at least two kinds of memory. Some things you can recognize when the objects or ideas are put before you. Others you can recall at will. Hence, the psychologist says that you have recognition and recall memories.

There may be a third kind: subconscious memory—a fleeting, haunting vestige of some past experience which may not quite reach the threshold of consciousness. Your memory is searchlighting the obscure recesses of your mind. Thus you strive for some name which eludes you, feel triumphant when you bring it up to conscious level. A loud noise stirs fears buried deep in your subconscious heritage. You may feel uneasy while exploring a cave. Some of these subconscious memories may influence your behavior whether you realize it or not.

FOUR LAWS OF MEMORY

We hear, read, do, say or think something—then through repetition etch it upon our nervous system. We have built a memory.

Memory is much more than recalling names, dates, faces, places. Twenty years ago, I crushed a finger between two leaves of a garage door. I still recall the sickening sound of crushing bone, the queasy stomach, the horrible pain. Memories all.

I hadn't ridden a bicycle for 20 years when my adolescent

daughter challenged me to ride hers—which I did with great ease. The bicycle-riding memory, you see, had not been lost.

As a boy, I used to re-cane chairs for pin money. No doubt about it, I could do it to this day. Or roller skate, paddle a canoe, solve an algebraic equation (a simple one, please), repeat the preamble to the Declaration of Independence, identify the odor of the Chinese laundry where as a child I bought firecrackers, recall the taste of my mother's "shoo-fly" pie, remember the smoothness of my grandfather's big silver watch.

You, too, have thousands of similar memories, temporarily buried, but still available to recall. In addition, you have tens of thousands of memories buried so deep in the basic you that you can no longer instantly bring them to light. But they're still there, part of your fabric, just as the unseen cellulose cell is part of a bolt of cotton cloth. If memories are fugitive, separate, fragmentary, you'll have trouble using them; if they're related, integrated, vivid, you'll be able to recapture many of them.

Most of your memories begin as *external sensations*—things you see, hear, smell, touch, taste. Some memories arise from *bodily sensations* such as pain, hunger, thirst, sex, functional disorders, muscular activities. Still others emanate from *emotional states* of happiness or unhappiness. Finally, some memories come from *thought,* the imaginative or reasoned recombination of ideas already remembered.

Remember those four origins, please:

1. External sensory impressions.
2. Bodily sensations.
3. Emotional states.
4. Thought.

MEMORY SELECTION—THE FIRST LAW

It is basically true that you have little or no control over most of the activities, or stimuli, which touch your life. Yet you are not therefore like a marble in a box, being shaken by an unseen hand, touching other marbles briefly, with neither rhyme nor reason. This is so because you have the power of *selection:* You can (if you but will) choose many of the significant memories which shall enter your life.

Selection is the first law to be observed in putting memory to work for you. What will you do over the next hour? Read this book? Take a walk? Watch television? Go to the movies? Take a nap? Drink some coffee? Work in the garden?

What will you do over the next year? Join a new club? Take some course of study? Get married? Move into a new residence? Repair antique furniture? Take up golf?

As you choose, so you automatically choose the memories which will be yours. Selection requires decision. Even failing to choose anything is a selection. We have called selection a law; let's now express it affirmatively:

Law 1—Constantly seek out a course of action which seems to promise betterment for you.

Seems obvious, doesn't it? But you'll probably violate it a dozen times in the next 24 hours. Thus, you may choose to read the comics, instead of a technical magazine, listen to silly banter on television, instead of a serious economic discussion, guzzle soda pop and highly seasoned hot dogs instead of some more balanced diet, or indulge in a hate snit, instead of calm meditation.

Beginning to get the point? What you select slowly determines what you become—that is, what memories will rest in your store-house for future use.

Note that Law 1 doesn't merely require you to select a benign course of action from possibilities presented to you—it commands you to *seek it out.* You have to go after it. Not likely that a technical magazine, an economic discussion, proper food, or an hour of meditation will seek you out. But they're available to you if you seek them out.

You never thought, did you, that a chapter on memory would first place the burden on your shoulders? Yet it's true: frequently you remember what you *want* to remember. So we can upgrade our law into the following phraseology:

Law 1—*Strive to remember those things which seem to promise betterment for you.*

This way of putting it doesn't preclude the comics, but it suggests that you try to remember the technical magazine articles. Listen occasionally to the TV fluff, but hold on to the economic ideas. Pop and hot dogs infrequently, but a balanced diet, regularly. Righteous anger may be all right, if converted into constructive action. Choose to remember things which are good for you.

CONCENTRATION—THE SECOND LAW

The rays of a strong sun beat down upon a piece of paper, change it not at all. A child focuses those same rays through a magnifying glass—and the paper burns.

Concentration, the second law of memory. This law can be stated quite simply:

Law 2—Concentrate on what is to be remembered.

Selection, of itself, is a kind of concentration, but you need more than that. You need to exclude distractions and with as many senses as possible to attend to that which is to be remembered. Try to see it, hear it, touch it, taste it, and smell it.

Each sense reinforces the others, fills out the memory, keeps it longer in your storehouse, available for recall. If you can do so, create mental "pictures" of how it looked, sounded, felt, tasted, or smelled.

Let's see this law in action. You meet Mr. Harry Pierce. You hear his name, and say, "Pierce. Which way do you spell it?"

So you hear (and "feel") yourself saying his name. You feel the firm grasp of his hand, hear him spell out *P-I-E-R-C-E.* You see that he is tall, well built, dressed in a gray suit, has blond hair, a mole on his chin. You smell the strong odor of a pipe. These are concentrations on sensory impressions, the basic stuff of which most of your memories are made: bricks, but not mortar.

Or, again: You are going to meet a Swedish capitalist, want to become his American representative. So you read all you can find about Sweden, about his enterprise, his products; organize a notebook containing this information; draw maps, copy charts. You discuss these subjects with an educated Swede of your acquaintance. Next, you borrow colored talkies on Sweden, review them several times. You attend a permanent exhibit of Swedish manufactured products, handle them, talk with the guide. You learn Swedish currency, exchange rates, shipping practices, banking relationships.

When you get your interview with the Swedish industrialist, he is amazed at your knowledge (memory) of things Swedish. Oh, yes— you get the job, of course. Concentration pays off.

When you can reasonably do so, give your memory a chance to digest new ideas, before stuffing it with more. Thus, for example, if you wanted to study astronomy, you might get a tutor to give you: (1) one lesson at an eight hour session, or (2) eight lessons of an hour each, over eight weeks.

The second method would be better, because each new lesson would have a chance to sink in—that is, to become integrated or associated with your existing knowledge.

A good memory, like safety, is no accident. To acquire it, you have to work at it; to hold onto it, you have to keep working at it. All this chapter can do is to give you the four basic laws; whether you apply them in your life is up to you. So far, we have said:

1. Since you can't remember everything you encounter in your day-to-day living, you must select things which seem more important to your happiness and progress.
2. Next, you consciously concentrate on various angles or aspects of the things you have selected; noting with different senses their several attributes—how they look, sound, feel, taste and smell. Often it pays to concentrate on the circumstances surrounding the thing to be remembered: where were you; who were there; when was it; why should you try to remember?

ASSOCIATION—THE THIRD LAW

Your memories are not stored in your brain like hardware store items in bins. Rather they are like telephone subscribers, each one of which is potentially connected with all others through central switchboards (covered in Chapter 8). These connections we call "association"; they are like the wires between subscribers and switchboard. Here's the law:

Law 3—Associate new ideas with one another, and with present memories.

Let's go back to your first meeting with Harry Pierce. You concentrated to get a lot of impressions, noted some associations:

Ideas with one another	*Ideas with present memories*
Pierce–tall	Spells it differently from Dr. Pearce
Pierce–well built	His head would pierce the ceiling of our attic
Pierce–blond	He looks like Uncle Harry–and his name is Harry, too
Pierce–gray suit	Met him at the Athletic Club, we both were playing tennis
Pierce–mole on chin	
Pierce–piercing voice	

Some of these are associations of circumstance (met him at the club), some are of contrast (Dr. Pearce), some of similarity (piercing voice, pierce the ceiling, looks like Uncle Harry). Still others are associations by observation (tall, blond), that is, original impressions associated with a man named Pierce.

Association goes on with virtually all new things learned. A pre-existing set of many memories will permit numerous associations, which increases the length of time the new material will be recallable. Absence of a comprehending background means few associations, quick forgetting.

For example, you learn that Mozart had a perfect sense of pitch. If you already know things about "Mozart" and "perfect pitch" you'll remember this bit a long time–otherwise it will have little significance, will soon be forgotten.

Let's put this another way: The chances are that you and I, over our lifetimes, have been equally exposed to ideas concerning ballistics, as an example. Now, it happens that I have little interest or background in this subject, so that virtually none of my exposure has stuck. If you, on the other hand, were interested in physics, or firearms, or crime detection, your (equal) exposure to ballistics information might result in a considerable increase in memory along these lines. You would have integrated the new information into existing knowledge, through association. You, in other words, would remember the ballistics material.

We tend to remember longer those things which fit in with present memories or with present interests (needs, desires, motivations). Hence, with material you have selected, and concentrated on, you can improve retention by noting its benefits to you (interest associations) and its relationships to present knowledge (similarities, differences, circumstance).

Even assumed interest will help; that is, I might tell myself, "If another war comes, a knowledge of ballistics might help me, so I'll master it right now."

When events or ideas are associated with great emotionality (happiness or unhappiness) they will remain in memory longer than otherwise. You'll never forget your courtship, the loss of a loved one, your narrow escape from death. Vivid memories stick.

You see then, that if concentration supplies the bricks of which memory is made, association supplies the mortar which binds them together.

REPETITION—THE FOURTH LAW

I know a billiard expert who will practice various difficult shots hour after hour. He's teaching his muscles how to remember those shots.

A friend of mine can name any wine you put before him, just from a tiny taste. Some folks can similarly distinguish coffees or teas. These taste memories have been built up through hundreds of repetitions.

An old man in our community can recite whole acts of Shakespeare. (He's been wishing them on his friends at every opportunity for fifty years or more.) Repetition keeps these memories fresh.

Lamination means building up, layer by layer. Plywood board is a good example. Repetition provides lamination for your memory. Each repetition adds its own memory to the first one. So a memory acquires depth, a third dimension, a thickness on top of the original memory.

Let's see repetition in action. You read a humorous limerick (one impression, one memory). You chuckle at it, read it to some one else (more layers: seeing, hearing, saying). You decide to memorize it, read it again (another layer). Then you recite it aloud. Now you have it memorized. Twenty years later you'll still be able to recall it. So now for the fourth law:

Law 4—Repeat memories, to retain them. This fourth law holds for sensory and muscular memories as well as for ideas. For example: You remember what Abraham Lincoln looked like, because you have seen his picture repeatedly (sight). You can identify the voice of (i.e., remember the sound of) your favorite TV commentator, because you have heard him so often (sound). Can you imagine (recall) the taste of orange juice? Drinking these juices repeatedly built up those memories. An Eskimo might not possess them (taste). Can you reach into a pocketful of change and draw out a dime? The feel of that coin again and again has kept its memory sharp (touch). Burning leaves in the fall—what a memory! Yet you did not have it when you were one year old. Again, repetition year after year has kept the smell memory alive (smell). Can you recall the "feel" of roller skating, paddling a canoe, batting a baseball, skipping rope? You did those things so many times that you can still remember them (muscular).

> My old friend Mye Walters runs a most unique secretarial school. Its graduates take prizes in national contests, command big salaries, hold important jobs, operate as court stenographers. "How did you do it, Mye?" I asked him. "It's survival-of-the-fittest," he explained. "We graduate only 20 percent of those who enroll. Our training includes four hours' practice five days a week for ten months. We drill 'em in shorthand until they can take notes faster than the normal person can talk. They practice on the typewriter until they can make the machine sound like a machine gun." He laughed. "Those who survive that much practice have got to be good!"

Repetition was my friend's key to memory success. Selection, concentration, association—these played their parts, of course. But repetition—drill—practice—produced those fantastically rapid shorthand artists.

As a lesson in applied repetition, let us here repeat the four basic laws of memory.

Law 1—Strive to remember those things which seem to promise betterment for you.

Law 2—Concentrate on what is to be remembered.

Law 3—Associate new ideas with one another, and with present memories.

Law 4—Repeat memories to retain them.

Let's repeat it another way:

Law 1–Selection.
Law 2–Concentration.
Law 3–Association.
Law 4–Repetition.

Or perhaps we could so engrave these ideas upon your mind that they would leave a permanent

S
C
A
R

on your memory!

So, now, in one mnemonic word–SCAR–you have a way of remembering the four laws of memory. At this point, please close this book and repeat the four laws. Try it.

FORGETTING

The child who defined memory as "the thing you forget with" hit the nail right on the head. "Forgetory" is the enemy of memory.

Forgetting is a gradual process. It's not like turning off an electric light: one moment it's light, the next moment it's dark. Rather it is like the slow settling of a log into a swamp: the new memory sinks deeper and deeper, until finally it is buried (i.e., forgotten).

Experiments have shown that there is a curve of forgetting (see Figure 13). This curve reveals that most of the forgetting occurs soon after the original impression, after which the rate of losing a memory slows up.

For example, you meet ten people at an evening affair. Before you get into bed you have lost the names of five of them, can remember the faces of seven. The next day you can recall the names of but three, the faces of five. On the following day, you can recall the names of two, the faces of four. Obviously, the time to try remembering is soon after the original impression, when most of the forgetting occurs.

So after your host has introduced you to a person (that's selection), you concentrate and associate (as outlined with Mr. Pierce,

FIGURE 13
Curve of forgetting (showing percentage remembered after given periods of time)

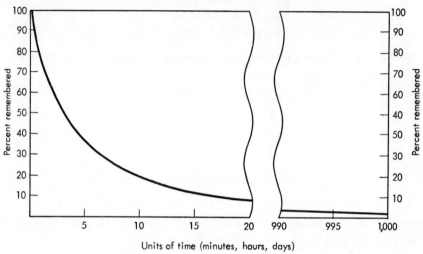

Units of time (minutes, hours, days)

above). You repeat his name in talking to him, or say it to yourself as you look at him. Again, and again over the evening, you do these same things, so that when you are ready to go home, you can call each person by his name, although you forget one name on the way home.

Psychologists say you can double your memory for any one thing, merely by repeating it three times. For example, read aloud the names of these two gangsters: Clarence G. Gaffray–Willard R. Penlam.

These two men were recently tried for murder. Willard R. Penlam claimed that he was innocent, but the prosecution produced evidence that Willard R. Penlam was actually the brains of a murder trust.

Now–close this book, and state the names of the two gangsters.

The chances are high that you couldn't recall the first name at all, but easily recalled the thrice-repeated name of Willard R. Penlam. If you remembered both names, try recalling them when you arise tomorrow morning. The name of Willard R. Penlam is more likely to stick.

Try hard to imprint originally. However, you can try too hard to recall. If you can't capture that name, or phone number, charge your mind with the obligation to recall it, then do something quite different for awhile. Often the wanted item will suddenly pop into your mind. You will have put your subconscious to work for you.

TWELVE MEMORY DEVICES

There are numerous devices which you can use to bolster your memory. Here are some of the most common:

1.   A name book. Purchase an A to Z pocket notebook, or use the same one as suggested for improving your vocabulary. Enter in it the names of people you meet. Review it from time to time, recalling faces, circumstances, incidents.
2.   A calendar pad or engagement book. Enter time and place of future dates.
3.   A tickler file. File material or reminders by future date, so that they will come to your attention when you'll want to review them. (But remember each day to look in your tickler file!)
4.   Underline significant passages in magazines and books (that belong to you), especially in texts and technical works. Review your marked passages from time to time, as suggested in the previous chapter.
5.   Outline (headings, subheadings, etc.) masses of knowledge you want to master and remember (also suggested previously).
6.   Talk it over, teach, explain, debate, write about whatever the subject is that you want to retain.
7.   Diagram it, to show relationships among the component parts.
8.   Keep a scrapbook into which you will paste pertinent clippings, illustrations, case studies, references.
9.   Set up a filing folder for each subject of interest. Select and file pertinent material.
10.   Master whatever techniques are applicable to the field of your interest.
11.   Associate with people who have a similar interest, especially with those who know more about it than you do.

12. Build a hobby around it—collecting items, producing handicraft, assembling exhibits, trying your hand at creation or
invention.

Figure 14, "Your Memory—It's Important," gives you a way to
look at your own memory development. Where you rate yourself
low, what will you do about it?

FIGURE 14
Your memory—it's important

In each of the ten lines below, check the block which comes closest to your self-appraisal. If you can't decide between two blocks, check the narrow space between them. Be honest, but not harsh with yourself!

Factor	2	3	4	5	6	7	8	9	10
Information	My general information is quite limited		I have a smattering of varied knowledge		I'm well informed in a few subjects		I keep consciously adding to my knowledge		I have vast knowledge, well organized
Reading	Other than newspapers I rarely do any reading		I am a very slow reader		I read newspapers, magazines, and novels		I read to add to my education		I read rapidly and retain meaning
Job knowledge	I have little job knowledge		I'm slowly learning more		I get by but am still learning		More than average I believe		I have vast knowledge in my line of work
Selectivity	I've never thought about being selective		I'm careless about trying to remember		I remember important or unusual things		Sometimes I look into new subjects of interest		I carefully select what I want to remember
Memory for names	I'm very poor at this		I remember faces much better than names		Sometimes I can tie up a name with a face		I really try to remember names		I concentrate and associate to remember new names
Memory for words	I ignore new and strange words		I guess at meanings of strange words		I pick up new words from time to time		I try to use new words in conversation		I look up dictionary meanings of new words
Use of concentration	I'm so confused, I can't concentrate		I'm not very observant		If it interests me, I'll concentrate		I'm trying to learn to concentrate better		I concentrate hard on things I must learn
Taking notes	I seldom bother to make notes		No need in my life to make notes		Occasionally I make notes as necessary		I record important items regularly		I maintain a pocket memo book
Orderly filing	My papers are usually unfiled and disorderly		I have no particular system		I have places for important things		I'm systematic and orderly		I maintain an adequate filing system
Tickler system	I don't even know what a "tickler system" is		I have no need for it		I keep track of obligations in my head		I use a calendar pad for this		I use an organized tickler system

11

Let your imagination work for you

Imagination—is it fugitive mental images like those in a kaleidoscope; fantasies far removed from the real world; capricious flights of fancy; creativity? It can be all these things, of great, or little value to you, *as you elect.* It roams the shadowland between your conscious and subconscious minds. It has some substance, but at the same time it is the stuff from which your dreams are made.

An inspiring idea, once awakend will not again slumber, although it may lurk in some shadowy corner of your mind. More likely, it will illuminate it. Don't arbitrarily reject it as impractical, for you may actually be close to some future reality.

John Dewey, perhaps the greatest philosopher our country has produced, wrote, "The imagination is not necessarily . . . the unreal. The proper function of imagination is vision of realities that cannot be exhibited under existing conditions of sense perception. Clear insight into the remote, the absent, the obscure is its aim: Imagination supplements and deepens observation."

ADVERSITY MAY GIVE
BIRTH TO CREATIVITY

An ancient adage declares that necessity is the mother of invention. Under adversity, imagination may be called upon to meet a challenge. The president of a corporation recently said to me, "One thing good about a business recession—it sure breeds innovation."

Most of us wait until we are face to face with some difficult situation, before we try to solve it, often under some time pressure. However, many, though not all, problems can be foreseen; that is, imagined before they occur. Your self-same imagination can create possible solutions or alternate courses of action.

Here are some exercises in imagination: what will you do if you're laid off from your job? Technology is obviously going to make your job unnecessary? You have to, or want to, seek another job? You should master some new skill, or subject of study? You are offered a better job, but in a distant locality? You want to cultivate some more cultured friends? You suffer a severe heart attack?

From time to time, you may have casually wondered about these, and other, possible changes in your life. Don't just wonder— rather, think through just how you would meet these situations and what would be the results in your life style.

Finally, are your proposed answers stodgy and timid or imaginative and courageous? Realize that genuine progress consists of discovering the new, not just in rediscovering the old.

WANT TO BE A GENIUS?

There are many definitions of genius, but the one I like best is found in the Journal of Henri-Frederic Amiel, a 19th-century writer: "Doing easily what others find difficult is talent; doing what is impossible for talent, is genius."

> Beethoven was a piano virtuoso as well as a composer. Following a brilliantly played concert, a woman admirer said, "If God had only given me that gift of genius." Beethoven replied, "It is not genius, madam. All you have to do is practice on your piano 8 hours a day for 40 years." The great pianist, Paderewski, called a genius, said, "Before I became a genius I was a drudge."

Here then, is one key to genius—perseverance in your chosen field. In the case of both musicians, practice yielded perfection in sensory-motor coordinations.

Sometimes genius is purely in the realm of thought.

> Alexander Hamilton was lauded as the genius who financed the American Revolution. He commented, "When I have a subject in hand, I

study it profoundly. Day and night it is before me. My mind becomes
pervaded with it. Then the effort which I have made is what people are
pleased to call the fruit of genius. It is the fruit of labor and thought."

Labor and thought! Not a scintillating flash of rare mystical wisdom, but just common clay—labor and thought, such as you and I
can produce. If you half suspect that you are a genius, try just
plain plugging away, instead of waiting for some startling inspiration.

Maybe now you don't want to opt for genius, will settle for
being a person of high talent in some one field of endeavor. Even
so, you'll still find two items on the price tag—labor and thought.

THE "IF I WERE" GAME

In the successful stage play *Fiddler on the Roof,* the main male
character sings "If I were a rich man," and tells what he would do.
You yourself can play this fantasy game with great benefits possible. In a quiet half hour think what you would know, do, be, if
you were your boss (having to supervise the likes of you!); your
spouse (married to what you know yourself to be); your child
(craving to respect you as a parent).

A bit scary, isn't it? Your imagination can be a mirror in which
you see yourself as others see you, but it can also serve as a crystal
ball in which you see yourself as you would like to be. Then you
can ask yourself what you would have to know—do—be—, if you
were . . . .

BRAINSTORMING

In business, some managers have fostered "brainstorming."
Under it, experienced employees are brought together for a freewheeling session to consider possible solutions to a problem. Suggestions, no matter how improbable are evaluated; some are
selected for testing in practical situations.

You can conduct your own brainstorming session by

1. Writing out some one problem or objective.
2. Listing the things you should *do, know,* and *be* to solve the
   problem, or achieve the objective.

3. Don't avoid the unusual, the difficult, or the bizarre in your list. This is where your imagination comes into play.
4. After each item listed, put a deadline for its accomplishment. Check it off when it's done.

By the time you've checked off the last item, the storm should be over, the skies sunny.

YOUR SIXTH SENSE

In Chapter 9 we noted that some folks seem to possess a "sixth sense"—also known as intuition or subconscious perception. Psychologists note evidence of its presence, but unlike Ben Franklin who, with his kite demonstrated the existence of electricity, they have been unable to prove that the sixth sense exists.

The ability is more highly developed in some people than in others. For some decades, Duke University has been the center for extrasensory perception research. Ridiculed at the outset, the studies ultimately confirmed that some people do, indeed, possess perceptive powers beyond the usual five senses. One controlled experiment revealed (1) that those with high ESP scores tended to be relaxed and self-assured; and (2) that those same high-scoring persons, when subjected to mental stress, lost much of their intuitive powers.

It is believed that in some way your *subconscious* takes in impressions from the outside world and from your own nervous system, processes them, and formulates a nebulous conclusion which you probably call a "hunch."

SOME FOLKS ARE PLAIN LUCKY!

—Or so it seems when Lady Luck smiles on them and scowls at you. Is it pure coincidence—sheer luck?

If you toss two dice enough times you will get as many 2s as 12s, and more 7s than any other number. That's because 7 can be made by 6 + 1, 5 + 2, 4 + 3, 3 + 4, 2 + 5, and 1 + 6—more combinations than for any other number. Let's suppose you don't know this fact, and your betting opponent does. Will it be luck if he scoops up the winnings?

Or, suppose you both own stock in a well-known company. He studies their quarterly reports, concludes that their ratio of current assets to current liabilities is going sour, and sells out. You, on the other hand, are content to accept the regular dividend checks, with a cursory glance at the net earnings per share. Ultimately you sell your stock at a loss. Was he lucky, you merely unlucky?

Psychologists have X-rayed Lady Luck, to reach certain conclusions. These are:

1. You are responsible for much of your luck, good or bad.
2. A defeatist attitude dulls your perception and judgment of events and opportunities. If you believe that the odds are against you in some undertaking, you'll probably prove yourself right.
3. Accident proneness is certainly one kind of bad luck. Psychiatrists believe (maybe have proven) that the condition frequently reflects an unconscious wish to punish yourself to ease some feeling of guilt.
4 When you are unhappy with yourself or suffering stress, "unlucky" things are more likely to happen to you.
5. Neurotic, highstrung people meet frustration with inadequate responses and so lessen their chances of successful outcomes (i.e., good luck). They likely see themselves as born losers.
6. Some people enjoy bad luck—health miseries, hard luck stories as conversation pieces—and gleefully recount their deficiencies. This self-flagellation is like a hairshirt to a religious zealot.
7. "Lucky" folks, by exercising sound judgment, optimism, courage and self-confidence continue to be lucky.

How about you? Do you believe No. 1 above? Will you adopt No. 7? Or are you enmeshed in Nos. 2, 3, 4, 5 and 6?

IMAGINATION THE SAME AS CREATIVITY?

Your imagination, creativity, intelligence and education—are they much the same thing?

No—although admittedly there is overlapping among them. In this chapter we are endeavoring to show you how to use your imagination, education, and intelligence to become more creative. Imagination is an all-inclusive term which can include fantasy, dreams, reveries, Castles-in-Spain, conceptual understanding, estheticism, artistic expression, inspiration, inventiveness, freewheeling thought, visualization, wishful thinking, and subconscious revelations.

All these terms represent intangible concepts; the meaning of any one is likely to be what you think it is. Your interpretation of it may differ from mine. Hence, we shall use a definition of imagination which is somewhat restricted: Imagination is the ability to form mental images of that which is not currently, or cannot be, comprehended by sensory perceptions. If you can see it, hear it, feel it, taste it, smell it, you don't need to imagine it. Artists, writers, poets, architects, inventors, research scientists, social leaders and explorers frequently utilize high imagination.

If the exercise of imagination produces some *novel* result (painting, story, poem, structure, machine, scientific principle, human program, or geographic finding) the imaginer is said to be *creative*.

Either pure imagination, or applied imagination (creativity) can utilize factual knowledge (education) and intellect (memory, reasoning, words, etc.) to get results or to reach conclusions.

WHAT IS CREATIVITY?

Creativity, then, is the effort which produces a new and/or better product or solution. Imagination typically sires the effort and indeed supplies much of the emotion power for it, by foreseeing the probable benefits or rewards.

The product can be tangible, such as a transistor or atomic bomb; or intangible such as the theory of relativity or a treaty among nations.

Creativity, then, can be with physical things, as the invention of the steam engine; ideas, such as the concept of democracy by our Founding Fathers; social relationships, such as depicted by an organization chart. Often, creativity combines two, or all three of these areas.

The inventiveness mothered by necessity is rarely of a high order. The child who puts a telephone book on a chair so that he can reach the cookie jar is ingenious, but scarcely creative.

True creativity flourishes in an encouraging environment, shrivels up under restrictions, criticism, or gloom. If your mind is incandescent with innovative dreams, nourish them tenderly. Don't let discouragement, defeat or the treadmill of daily living cause the heat to diminish, the light to flicker, so to reduce the burning dreams to dying embers.

HOW YOU CAN BECOME MORE CREATIVE

Creative persons usually are super-talented in one field of endeavor. The world has seen few such as Leonardo da Vinci who, five centuries ago, was an outstanding painter, sculptor, engineer, astronomer and scientist. Or, Thomas Jefferson, who was a capable lawyer, statesman, writer, inventor, architect and violinist.

We have already noted that many individuals considered to be geniuses, modestly ascribe their performances to practice, practice, practice. However, they obviously possess more, else skilled jugglers and professional athletes would all be geniuses. Ideas—conceptual creativity—are needed: integration of known concepts into a new combination; or identification of an existing interrelationship (law or principle) which has been there all along but was unrecognized. Think of Isaac Newton and the law of gravity.

Four steps can make you more creative in attacking a problem which you have *very clearly defined:*

1. *Preparation,* whereby you assemble pertinent knowledge and classify it into some logical order. For creativity is part mirror, reflecting the knowledge of others, part candle, adding new light.

This preparation should preferably be in a narrow field with which you already have considerable familiarity.

> In industry there is a well developed technique for analyzing jobs, assigning them to various grade levels, and determining the pay limits of the grades. Ignoring this existing knowledge, many top managers arbitrarily establish their own job classification systems, frequently causing inequities in pay rates, with resulting labor trouble.

2. *Analysis,* whereby you study the material you have collected for similarities, differences, underlying principles or tentative conclusions.

At this stage, irrelevant material should be set aside. The very act of determining what material is *not* pertinent to your problem helps point your thinking toward some ultimate solution.

3. *Conclusion.* Your conclusion should be tentative. It may be the result of logic, whereby all other possibilities have been eliminated. It may be an inspiration, an illuminated leap of thought which hits you like a blinding light.

> Inspiration was the case with Greek Archimedes who, while bathing, suddenly realized how to measure the volume of an object by the water it displaces. "Eureka!" ("I have found it"), he exclaimed, a word which persists in our language to this day.

4. *Verification.* Once a problem has been solved or a conclusion reached, it must be tested to determine whether it fits all conditions, or has limited applicability, or must be expanded or contracted in phraseology.

This is the moment of truth which may make you a "genius," or an impractical analyzer of the particular problem at hand. If your first conclusion is inadequate, or even quite wrong, don't despair. Repeat the four steps here given—and in greater depth.

IMAGINEERING

"Imagineering" is a coined word which means engineering the power of your imagination so that it accelerates your advancement.

You are the unique possessor of knowledge, experience, and fugitive fantasies. Most of these concepts plod on to logical thought and orderly procession in your life. But some ideas are like scampering children playing hide and seek. By joining reasoning with imagination, you have the potential to create concepts and things not possible for others who have different backgrounds. Whether you will put this potential to work for you, or ignore it, you alone can decide.

Previously, we have spelled out the procedure to become more creative: preparation, analysis, conclusion, verification. These are mechanistic, and need the leavening influence of imagination at all four stages. Do not be afraid of dreams, flights of fancy, impossibilities, fantasies, wild assumptions. As soon as a new idea crystallizes, hold it in your mind's eye, or record it on paper for later use.

Imagineering takes time. You are not likely to produce some brilliant idea just because you want to. Get additional information. Let loose your subconscious upon the problem. Consciously think about it. Accept or reject, based on what you consider the ultimate goal. Change that goal, or get it in clearer focus. Chip away, like a sculptor carves a block of marble—a bold stroke here, a delicate tap there.

Ultimately, reasoning takes over. You capture your wayward birds of fancy and organize them under logical headings, such as the classic what, how, when, why, where and who; or as guiding principles, near-term action, and long-range goals.

If unsolved questions remain, let your subconscious wrestle with them. Some morning, early, the answers will startle you into wakefulness. Then you need no longer float in imagination's stratosphere; you can parachute from the clouds down to a practical test of your solution. But should you meet defeat, don't despair—back to the clouds again.

12

Overcoming stress

Psychosomatics tells us that our emotional stresses cause many of our physical problems. And vice versa. These findings are the results of years of research into psychosomatics. Doctors assert that more than 50 percent of the illnesses they treat have been emotionally induced. A Cornell Medical Center report concluded that "all diseases . . . are influenced by the sick person's adaptation to his environment."

Per contra: emotional maturity causes physical well being; good health promotes mental peace.

You can either control your negative emotions—or they can become sinister ogres which threaten your happiness. The choice is yours. This book tells you how to take charge of your emotions. The knowledge can make you free.

PSYCHOSOMATICS

An emotion, as William James defined it is "A state of mind that manifests itself by sensible changes in the body." Without these chemical and/or physical changes in muscles, heart, blood-vessels, digestive tract and ductless glands, there would be no emotion, either pleasant or unpleasant.

> Some years ago I was caught in a large retrenchment program of my corporate employer. When my boss broke the bad news, a wave of heat

instantly suffused my body and I felt a bursting pressure in my head. Had I been 30 years older, I would likely have suffered a stroke.

To understand psychosomatics, recall that your body has two types of nervous system: (1) *conscious*—brain, spinal cord, plus sensory nerves (incoming sensations), motor nerves (outgoing orders to muscles and some body organs) and associative (connecting) nerves; and (2) *unconscious*—an internal nerve system (also called sympathetic, and autonomous) which controls heartbeat, lung action, digestion, chemical balance, ductless (endocrine) glands and many other body functions. It can stimulate, depress, or maintain these functions in balance. In addition, it can receive "messages" from or transmit them to, the conscious system. Research indicates that man may be able to exert some control over this internal nervous system (biofeedback).

Of further interest to us here are certain powerful ductless glands: (1) the pituitary, situated in the center of your skull, and (2) two adrenal glands, one attached to each kidney. Figure 15 presents a diagrammatic representation of the locations of these important glands.

FIGURE 15
Pituitary and adrenal glands

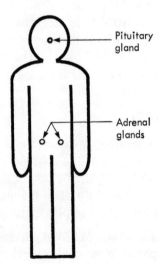

Pituitary gland

Adrenal glands

RESEARCH BY DR. SELYE

Dr. Hans Selye, an Austrian-born Canadian, has done extensive research into the role of hormones in meeting stress—the wear and tear of everyday living. Noting that stress of one sort or another is the lot of mankind, he points out that it:

1. Can be defined as "the nonspecific response of the body to demands made upon it." Thus, being ill "all over" is nonspecific, regardless of some specific cause. As a young medical student Selye had noted that the early symptoms of many illnesses were similar. In later research, he demonstrated that much the same bodily reactions occurred, no matter what the cause of stress was: infection, injury, unhappiness, challenge, time pressure, and so forth.

2. Can be benign or harmful—the spice of life, as in great joy, or bitter misery as in hate, fear or guilt.

3. Depends less on what actually happens than on how you react to it—that is, your adaptation to what activities you undertake or to what is done to you.

4. Results from what he terms an "alarm reaction," whereby you become aware of some (real or fancied) threat or danger. Some examples: a severe blow, loss of a job, death of a loved one, food poisoning, criticism, defeat.

Typically, stress follows a certain sequence:

1. There is an awareness of danger, real or fancied; or of some important change in your life. This is the "alarm reaction."
2. Exciter hormones, which prepare the body for fight or flight, are secreted by several ductless glands. Sometimes these hormones merely help to accept or adjust.
3. Quieter hormones, designed to restore equilibrium (i.e., emotional tranquility) are then secreted. Should the stressor persist, balance will not be restored, resulting in—
4. Fatigue, ultimately in exhaustion. We see then that worry, apprehension, indecision or continuing frustration can deplete your energy.

> After 22 years' service, 48-year-old Cary was given two months' severance pay when his employer went bankrupt. Within three days, he couldn't summon enough energy to get out of bed, felt himself a failure, contemplated suicide. Then his old boss got financial backing for a new

company and asked Cary to join him. The very next day, Cary started
the new job, full of hope and renewed energy.

Stress, long endured, can autograph your will as well as your
face. Additionally, it can make your body susceptible to a variety
of ailments: muscle tension, headaches, insomnia, indigestion, high
blood pressure, heart attacks, strokes, sinusitis, allergies, kidney
disease, arthritis, indigestion, ulcers, spastic colon, and others. (It's
not what you eat that gives you ulcers, it's what's eating you.) On
the other hand, the healthy body with a healthy mind lives in
peace, unaware of normal internal changes.

Your response to a given stressor will vary with different stages
of your life and different cultural backgrounds. Consider, for
example, loss of a job by (1) a 16-year-old boy who still attends
school; (2) a 26-year-old married man with three dependents; (3) a
56-year-old man with a large income from investments; (4) a
trained nuclear engineer 40 years old; (5) an unskilled common
laborer, 50 years old, with low education. Although the stressor
might be the same, its impact on these five individuals would likely
be very different.

The human body seems unable to distinguish between physical
and mental stressors, whether they represent losses, threats or even
ecstasy. If you cut your finger, the exciter-quieter sequence works
well to resist infection and then to heal the wound. The same pattern occurs in a sudden fright, a mental stressor.

Unknown to you, your body is continuously resisting bacteria
and viruses which assail it. An overwhelming stressor can temporarily halt this resisting capability, laying the body open to infection. A prolonged stressor can bring on fundamental organic problems of a serious nature. There is even some evidence that suscep-
tibility to cancer can in part be attributed to dejection, hopelessness, and years of feeling worthless.

Anxiety is a steady stream of fear which etches a mind channel
that sluices away all other thoughts. If such a mental stressor
continues—fear of losing a job, for instance—futile overproduction
of quieter hormones can reduce the resistance of the entire body
to infection or to other genuine physical stressors. We have all
observed that highly neurotic people become heir to many physical
ailments. Continued mental stress destroys health (equilibrium) and

so leads the way to a host of functional and, ultimately, organic problems.

An emotionally overwrought person is a sick person. If his distress worsens, or merely continues unabated, a hospital bed awaits him.

FIGHT OR FLIGHT

Psychologists tell us that we either attack our problems, or run away from them (fight or flight). Physiologists tell us that the body tries to follow the same pattern in its reactions to stressors.

In the alarm stage there is first a tendency toward withdrawal, as the fighting troops (the excitor hormones) are called up. In the resistance stage, the troops get to work: germs are killed by antibodies; fear of an antagonist is overcome by courage. Normally, the battle is soon over; the troops have been victorious! The quieter hormones can hold their banners high as they clean up the battlefield. However, if the battle continues, flight may finally win out— the germs multiply, or the individual tries to run away from his enemy. There are no reserve troops, no more victorious banners; only exhaustion of the bodily activities, which may lead to serious illness, a broken personality, or death.

While this description is fanciful, it nevertheless depicts a very usual process when the body must contend with a long-continued internal or external stressor.

ADAPTATION

The hormone system of your body is an adaptation system, designed by nature to meet the stresses of day-to-day living, primarily by fight or flight. It worked well for the survival of primitive man, when the stressors were largely external: wild animals, human enemies, and natural forces.

In civilized societies, these external forces only occasionally are your stressors. More frequently you face self-generated mental stressors—various kinds of hate, fear, and guilt. Adaptation to these stressors is not automatic—you have to understand them and learn how to meet them. Since they are mostly subjective-caused they can usually be subjective-cured.

A useful form of adaptation is substitution. Here are some examples: You are worried about the illness of a loved one—cut down a tree or shovel show. You feel depressed—whistle or sing. You have been defeated in an election for some office—get a turkish bath. An acquaintance has doublecrossed you—organize a group for some game.

What you do may bear no relationship at all to the stressor. The important point is that you *do* something, preferably an action which involves the large muscles of the body. For a while, at least, you will stop brooding and so help to restore hormonal balance.

Your attitudes are the windows through which you interpret your environment. Changing your actions may change your attitudes and so brush away some of the fog from your windows.

The process of adapting to radical change is psychologically painful. A new job, moving to a new community, divorce, adjusting to the death of a loved one or embracing a different religion—all these require difficult adjustments. For some, if the wrench is too severe, a "nervous breakdown" ensues, characterized by anxiety, guilt, depression, and perhaps apathy. With acceptance of the changed situation, these personality disorders will normally lessen or disappear altogether.

In the adjustment period, you may be Dr. Jekyll and Mr. Hyde (schizophrenic, the psychiatrists call it). Here you try to accept two opposing beliefs, hang on to the old order while embracing the new, try to live with divided loyalties, slide down both sides of the fence. In the normal person, one or the other wins out, the dilemma is resolved and the conflict recedes.

NEGATIVE STRESSORS

Here's a list of some common negative stressors capable of setting off your alarm reactions:

Physical—a heavy blow; an accident; excessive noise; glaring light; extreme cold or heat; offensive odors; bitter taste; pain; dizziness; malfunctioning of body. The last three can be effects as well as causes.

Intellectual—lack of needed information; failure of memory; inadequate vocabulary; mathematical error; puzzle; complex problem; anxiety; indecision; conflict of ideas.

Social—rejection by peers or superiors; criticism; inadequate acceptance by a group; loneliness; disagreement with group standards; low income; few possessions; divided loyalties; losing your job.

Emotional—principally caused by hate, fear, and guilt, which will be discussed in a later chapter. Also religious conflicts; low self-image.

Lasting wounds can result from losing your job. There can result a feeling of worthlessness, a change in life-style or disaffection with the social order. The hurt can be especially acute if you feel that the job loss was unjustified. These psychological wounds can in turn induce spastic colons, stomach ulcers, heart attacks, or other psychosomatic disorders. Once an individual has lost what he considers a good job, he will carry a lurking apprehension that it could happen again.

Based on a study of 3,000 men and women, a German psychiatrist concluded that one year of unemployment reduced the life expectancy of a worker by as much as five years, in part due to marital discord and the use of alcohol and drugs brought on by the unemployment.

TYPE A BEHAVIOR

Related to negative stressors is Type A behavior. Researchers have discovered that aggressive, hostile, overly ambitious, harried "go-getters" are more prone to coronary heart attacks than the average person. These individuals, exhibiting Type A behavior, engage in a constant battle with *time,* substituting repetitive urgency for creative energy. Sometimes they are monsters of egotism.

The Type B person, on the other hand, is unhurried and patient. He may be just as ambitious to get ahead as Type A, but his approach to problems is more leisurely and confident, albeit persevering. He can play and relax without a guilty feeling that he's wasting precious time.

If you recognize that you show many Type A symptoms, you will be wise to slow down. Avoid self-imposed, hard-to-meet deadlines. Curb impatience with yourself and others. Don't interrupt or finish sentences for other people, or ram your opinions down their throats. Listen—don't hog the conversation. Avoid pet hates. Speak calmly, not vehemently. Eat at a leisurely pace. Take time for relaxation. Consciously relax neck, shoulder, arm, forehead and abdominal muscles. Also, avoid frequent contact with other Type As. Seek out the Bs.

ACCIDENT REPEATERS

Probably you have already observed that some people are accident prone. Safety directors in industry call them "repeaters." A report on accident-prone individuals, published in the *Journal of the American Medical Association,* stated that they tended to reveal frequent sexual conflicts, aggression, impulsiveness, anxiety, irresponsibility, frustration, fear, boredom and loneliness.

Those studied changed jobs frequently, often had childless marriages, revealed a high divorce rate, and were likely to be in conflict with the law or other authority. In some individuals, there seemed to be an unconscious attempt to gain attention and sympathy. These various attributes and actions are maladjustments, many (most?) of them brought on by negative attitudes.

When you are enmeshed in some negative emotional state, judgment, sensory perceptions and muscular coordinations are likely to be out of kilter—hence you are at that time accident prone.

OVERCOMING YOUR BOREDOM

Like the ordinary cold, boredom is a common complaint. Millions of industrial workers suffer from it. So do many housewives, clerks, soldiers in peace time, government employees, unemployed teenagers, leisure surfeited socialites, business executives, retirees.

In short, boredom can slowly engulf you, even as a low-lying fog rolls over you. Like the common cold, it can be infectious, spreading through a family, a classroom, or an employee group. Occasional boredom serves as an interlude between interesting activities, but continuing boredom devastates the human ego, and may lead to hostility, escapism, or destructiveness.

The cause of boredom is understimulation from environment,

people, or self. Folks vary widely in their boredom tolerance, and in the things which bore them.

If your life is boring you, get out of your rut. Do something new, different, stimulating, challenging. Study a new subject, learn a new skill, take up a new sport, change your daily routine, meet some new people, help some unfortunates. If these moves fail, candidly analyze your whole life-style—job, spouse, home life, community, beliefs, and future goals. Consciously look for things to change.

Even a slight change, without radically altering your life-style, can help. Go to bed later, or earlier, than at present. Take a bus to work instead of driving your car. After the evening meal, sit in another chair than customary, or in another room. Study the textbooks brought home by your teenage son.

TIME OUT TO RELAX

The stresses and strains of everyday living cause unconscious muscular tension: tightness in the shoulders, clenched fists, movements of the feet, quivering legs, tense abdominal muscles or a furrowed brow. Are you suffering from any of these *right now*?

By giving thought, you can consciously relax most of the large muscles of your body. Go limp as a wet cloth. When you do, the muscles telegraph to the brain, "All's well here." On the other hand, when muscles are tense, the telegraphed message reads, "Something wrong here. Send the fighter troops."

Deliberately take time out to relax, especially when you are under emotional stress. Do absolutely nothing for five or ten minutes. Push problems from your mind by introducing memories of pleasant events, colors, art forms, aromas, music or people. Soon, some amount of energy will resurge within you. Pursuit of some interesting hobby can yield the same result.

Transcendental meditation (TM) is a successful form of mental relaxation which has been practiced by Hindus for many centuries. American advocates assert that possibly 500,000 Americans currently are practicing TM. To practice it, for 20 minutes twice each day you "tune out," or get away from, distractions, close your eyes, and focus your mind on some sound which has no meaning, called a "mantra." Let your mind float and your muscles relax, much as in deep sleep—yet it is "restful alertness." At various locations around our country there are classes to teach TM as practiced by the Hindus. If you find you cannot meditate "on your own" you may want to find out if such a training program is available nearby.

Converted skeptics report fewer feelings of tension, work performed with less effort, greater productivity, a longer "fuse" under pressure, less worry, less defensiveness and better interpersonal relationships with others. We shall discuss TM again in Chapter 16.

Sounds too good to be true, you say. It works. Don't take my word for it. Try it sincerely, and without any preconceived notion—but follow it regularly for at least three months. It may not change your problems, but it may drastically alter the way you approach them.

BIOFEEDBACK

A promising development in mind-body interaction is biofeedback, also known as sensory feedback. Under it, an individual learns to control or to modify some function of his body over which he formerly had no conscious control.

To measure control, the technique uses electronic sensors which are attached to the part of the body where control is being attempted. The sensors pick up minute electrical activity within muscles, galvanic skin responses, heartbeat, blood flow, and temperature changes and convert the sensed activity to sounds or visual signals. By concentrated thought, the patient usually succeeds in controlling the feedback; that is, changing the sounds or signals, so that the harmful condition is eased.

Doctors report high percentages of success in biofeedback treatment of migraine headaches, insomnia, asthma, muscle paralysis and other neuromuscular disorders.

FAITH HEALING

Faith healing has been practiced by mankind for many centuries. Tribal medicine men cured their ailing members or calmed their troubled emotions, using mysterious rites, strange incantations, or entrails of animals. Organized religions believe in prayer, faith, confession, and the laying on of hands. Modern psychic healers sometimes bring about results which medicine has failed to accomplish. Their subjects assert that they feel eerily "out of this world," with energy vibrations coursing through their bodies. Physicians themselves may bring about "miracles" by prescribing placebos (sugar pills). Genuine hypnosis is a useful medical tool in certain conditions.

Underlying these various healing methods is *belief* by the patient that he will be helped. "Faith is the substance of things hoped for," says the Old Testament. Presumably the belief establishes some benign hormonal condition which the subject focuses on the affected organ or problem.

The medical profession is making serious studies of psychic healing, hoping to add to its growing body of psychosomatic knowledge, and knowing that many ailments clear up regardless of what the doctor does. In ancient Greece, the physician was first a philosopher, second a healer. Today, medical specialists may fail to realize that a human being is more than the sum total of his anatomy. Psychosomatics tells him to deal with the whole man— the intangibles as well as the tangibles.

YOUR STRESS

You can get some idea of your reaction to pressures upon you (stress) by checking the 20 items in Figure 16. If some of these items do not apply, substitute comparable items.

After you have interpreted your total score, study the items where you rated yourself as either poor or fair, and consider what actions you will take to improve them.

FIGURE 16
Self-rating on personal stress

Following are 20 aspects of your job, family life and self-image which can affect your stress. Rate yourself on each item by placing a check mark in the appropriate rating column:

	Rating				
	Poor	Fair	Aver-age	Good	Excel-lent
Job					
1. Quality of supervision given you					
2. Challenge provided by your job					
3. Job satisfaction from your creativity					
4. Freedom from distasteful tasks					
5. Your qualifications for your job					
6. Opportunity for advancement					
7. Constructive criticism from superiors					
8. Compensation and fringe benefits					
9. Friendliness of fellow workers					
10. Praise or recognition given you					
Family life					
11. Peace in the home					
12. Freedom from family demands upon you					
13. Sex life					
14. Love and affection shown you					
15. Family financial condition					
Self					
16. Foreseeable health					
17. Hobby or relaxation					
18. Your emotional maturity					
19. Faith in your future					
20. Living up to your self-image					
Total					

To score yourself:
1. Total the checks in each column (must equal 20)
2. Allow 1 point for poor, 2 for fair, 3 for average, 4 for good, 5 for excellent
3. Total the points and refer to the following table:

Points	Interpretation
80 to 100	You are well adjusted, free from much stress
65 to 79	Try to overcome the few things troubling you
55 to 64	You're just getting by; watch out!
40 to 54	You need drastic changes in some attitudes
20 to 39	Sorry, but you're probably neurotic

13

You can't *capture* happiness

Children searching for an elusive "bluebird of happiness" is the theme of a delightful play for young people, written by Maurice Maeterlinck. Years later, Dr. Russell Conwell delivered his famous sermon, "Acres of Diamonds," so many times that with the proceeds he founded Temple University in Philadelphia. The play and the sermon have much the same theme: happiness is available to you on your own doorstep.

When *Scholastic Magazine* polled 52,000 high school students, asking, "What is your foremost aim in life?" the answers were:

Money	15%
Fame and prominence	10%
To serve society	16%
Personal happiness	59%

The first three are achievable by work or choice, but happiness is a state of mind which results from benign thoughts and actions. You can't reach out and capture it.

Happiness is a byproduct of your thoughts and actions—particularly the latter. It is not a goal like the finish line of a mile run.

Poor people think they'd be happy if they were rich. Sick folks, if they were well. Timid, if they had courage.

The plain truth is that money does not yield happiness; not all well people are happy; timid folks, unhappy; courageous heroes, happy.

In a lifetime of, say, 70 years, you will spend more than 400,000 waking hours. How many will be happy, how many unhappy, how many zilch? Only you can decide.

What makes you think you *deserve* happiness? What have you ever done, what are you doing currently, to earn more than a fleeting glimpse of it?

Throughout a year you live many lives—home, work, social, play, worship. One of these may yield you happiness, another unhappiness. Or vice versa.

Consider your "fireside" life. Is it replete with domestic bliss, or bickering discord? Do you look forward to going home, or manufacture excuses to get out of it? Love in the home is a song in the heart.

THE FOUR LAWS OF HAPPINESS

You go through each day trying to satisfy *wants*—physical, intellectual, emotional, social. Sometimes your attempts bring you satisfaction, sometimes dissatisfaction. Here are four situations, and their outcomes:

The want	What happens to it	The outcome
The want is felt	It is met	Satisfaction
The want is felt	It is not met	Dissatisfaction
The want is not felt	Circumstance forces action	Dissatisfaction
The want is not felt	There is no pressure for action	Mild satisfaction

Whether the want is hunger, thirst, sex, power, status, acceptance, recognition, possessions, or scores of other felt needs, the above analysis applies. Think back over some great satisfaction in your life, and some extreme disappointment; can you identify in each instance which one of the four situations existed?

When you become conscious of a want, it becomes a stressor. It incites to action designed to satisfy it. As we have already noted, the stressor causes ductless glands (principally pituitary and adrenals) to discharge exciter hormones into the bloodstream. This condition results in more rapid heartbeat, increased lung action, more blood to large muscles, sweating, discharge of blood sugar from the liver into the circulatory system, and other mobilizations for action.

If the outcome of the action is success, the quieter hormones are released, so restoring satisfying internal equilibrium. To repeat: If you want something and get it, you're happy. If you want something and don't get it, you're unhappy. If you don't want to do something, but are forced to, you're unhappy. If you don't want action, and are let alone, you're content (i.e., passively happy).

Frustration (unhappiness) occurs when you are unable to cope adequately with some obstacle or pressure in your life. These may result from the forces of nature (a hurricane, for a dramatic example); animal or vegetable life (a vicious dog, or weeds in your garden); other persons—the boss, fellow employees, your spouse; your own attitudes–fear, hate, and guilt.

SERENITY

If we can't find ecstatic happiness, most of us would settle for peaceful serenity—passive happiness.

We have mentioned the importance of domestic tranquility. Peacefulness in the home establishes positive affective waves which, expanding, can color all other hours. Researchers have demonstrated that many industrial accidents result from employees' worrying about home situations—criticism, nagging, deficiencies of children, financial problems, guilt.

Patience helps serenity; the patient person builds emotional reserves; the impatient one depletes them. We all must learn to tolerate difference in others, injustice, absence of affection, pain and suffering. Retaliation for real or fancied wrongs usually invites more conflict, solves nothing.

You can cultivate patience by taking the long-range view. The immediate vexation will recede in importance as time unfolds, but a flash of temper will probably generate yet another hurt. Mark Twain said, "Temper is what gets most of us into trouble. Pride is what keeps us there."

As you look around you, it will become evident that not all of life's failures live on skid row—some have impressive houses, large bank accounts, and wretched souls.

EXTROVERT ACTS

Most of us have more thoughtful thoughts than thoughtful deeds. Our good intentions just seem to fade away.

Giving money to charity is not true extroversion, unless you give your time and energy as well. Every day of your life you have opportunities for extroversion. Friendly words, supportive words, pedestal words, sympathy, appreciation, commendation—these are extrovert communications which bring happiness to *two* people. Why deny yourself your portion of this joy?

"Serendipity" is a coined word which means a happy but unexpected result from some activity.

Extrovert acts in human relations are frequently serendipitous: they bring about happy and unexpected results. This truth was known to Disciple Luke when he preached, "Cast thy bread upon the waters."

List some things you could *do* to make your life more extrovert. Then begin them.

CREATIVITY FOR HAPPINESS

Creativity can become a great source of happiness, whether it is exercised through things, ideas, or people. As an example of creativity in the realm of ideas, consider the case of John Milton:

> Milton is considered one of the greatest of English poets. At the age of 46 he became blind. Nevertheless, he continued his writing, producing *Paradise Lost* when he was 55 and *Paradise Regained* at the age of 63. He passed on at 66, after 50 years of writing.

It seems self-evident that John Milton must have derived great satisfaction from the creativity of a writing career.

Most of us have some streak of creativity in us. Find yours and develop it. You'll find happiness in it.

RULE OF THE ELITE

The rule of the elite says that an individual who attains great superiority in one area will tend to remain superior in that and related areas.

The brightest boy or girl in the class will shine intellectually as an adult. The skilled auto mechanic will probably reveal competence in machine tool and building trades. The speedy runner can become an excellent tennis player. The high school class president will be elected to high office in later life.

Let's apply this rule to you. If you develop yourself to *high proficiency* in some skill or area of knowledge, the chances are high that you will remain at or close to the summit in your chosen field. Note that the two words "high proficiency" are stressed. If you fail this part of the law, you are merely mediocre—like millions of others. It's your deal!

Consider how you can build on some of your already demonstrated outstanding traits. By the time you have finished this book, you will realize that you have more assets than you have suspected. In the next to last chapter, we'll ask you to "put it all together" so that you too will be one of the elite.

HAPPINESS FROM COURAGE

A young soldier defined courage as "being afraid, but going ahead anyhow." Courage is victory over fear, not the absence of fear.

Fear is nothing to be ashamed of; without it, the race would not have survived. As we saw in the previous chapter, it is an internally generated stimulus which can mobilize your physical forces for fight or flight. We shall analyze it further in the chapter which follows.

We normally think of courage as physical—facing up to a bully, rescuing a child from a burning building, facing a wild animal.

> Of a higher order is moral courage, the courage of your convictions. This was the kind displayed by the 56 signers of the American Declaration of Independence, who in 1776 mutually pledged their lives, their fortunes, and their sacred honor. In the war years which followed, 12 had their homes burned; 2 lost their sons; 5 were captured as traitors to the King and tortured until they died; 9 died of hardships or wounds in military service; 1 shipowner had his ships destroyed by the British navy; quite a few gave up their homes and went into hiding to escape capture.

Most of these men were well-to-do. Twenty-four were respected lawyers or judges; 11 were merchants, 9 were successful landowners. Lacking the courage of their convictions they could have avoided trouble—and you wouldn't be a free American today.

If you had been a representative to the first Continental Congress, would you have had the courage to sign the Declaration of Independence? Or do you suspect that you have more wishbone than backbone?

When courage is needed, and you summon it to victory, you "feel good inside," triumphant, happy about it. That's because you've marshalled your emotion power: your ductless glands. If the battle is indecisive, however, you are torn with conflicting emotions (hormones). Even if the outcome is defeat, you can adjust to that fact better than to prolonged indecision.

We have all known people who repeatedly took lickings from life, but managed to remain friendly and optimistic. That took courage.

We've all known their opposites, too!

HAPPINESS FROM WORK

Most of us spend a goodly portion of our adult lives doing some kind of task. Your worklife can contribute to, or detract from, your overall happiness. It is a joy or a burdensome duty, as you conceive it.

The high rate of labor turnover among industrial workers suggests discontent and constant search for the elusive bluebird of happiness.

Our consulting organization has conducted about 140 employee attitude surveys. The results are expressed as "morale indices" which have produced some interesting findings:

1. Women employees normally possess better morale than men. In any department where this is not found, we investigate.
2. New employees have better morale than those with five years' service. Apparently, it takes five years (of those who stick it out) for disillusionment to reach its low. After that, morale slowly rises.
3. The quality of foremanship provided has greater influence on morale than has working conditions.

Most of us are unhappy when we'd like to work but are forced to be idle. Witness unhappy retired oldsters, suicide among the unemployed, and crime among idle teenagers.

It is also true that many who hold jobs are unhappy in what they are doing. If you are one of them I suggest either: (1) getting into some kind of work which brings you satisfaction; marrying the right career can be as important as marrying the right mate, or (2) consciously making a better adjustment to your job, fellow workers, income, bosses, and company. Consider the *good* features of your work, and the people around you. Don't let the 10 percent bad overshadow the 90 percent good. Think how empty your life would be if you awakened each day to do-nothingness.

Every personnel manager can cite names of employees who have quit to take "a better job," but within a few months wanted their old jobs back.

Does money make you happy? Ask the idle rich. Ask the movie stars who pop tranquilizers into their mouths like peanuts. Almost a century ago, Henry Ward Beecher noted that, "Very few men acquire wealth in such a manner as to receive pleasure from it."

The price you pay for happiness in work is the struggle of dreams, the pain of sacrifice and the sweat of toil.

HAPPINESS IS PLAY

Have you forgotten how to play? Are you so emotionally bankrupt that you can't enjoy dancing, participation in a game, a contest of wits, friendly humor, or just some silly, childish activity?

Play is elemental; it releases benign hormones; it offsets worry. Learn how, anew, please.

> At one time I lived in a community where five couples of us celebrated ten birthdays a year. Husbands or wives would plan ingenious surprises. We'd give crazy little presents, accompanied by humorous doggerel. Each party was hilarious. At one of them, I hid a tape recorder. Toward the close of the evening, when I played it back, we belly-laughed at our own unbelievable antics. I still think back fondly to those parties.

All work and no play makes Jack more than just a dull boy—prolonged, it will make him a sick man.

Play is at its best when it involves both muscular activity and hilarity. But it can be more subdued as in cards, pool, monopoly, and so forth.

Strenuous sports should be suited to your age and physical condition. If you become reasonably tired, and have a chance to rest, you will derive benefit from the physical activity. Your eyes will be bright, your cheeks flushed, your voice animated, your head high. You'll "feel wonderful."

If play is not part of your life, it's not because you don't know what to do, but rather you don't do what you know you should do.

GIVE LOVE, GET HAPPINESS

In the mid-fifties, Dr. Smiley Blanton, a psychiatrist, wrote a book which made a great impression on my life. It was entitled *Love or Perish*. A quote on the jacket says, "For without love, we lose the will to live. . . . We may escape actual death, but what remains is a meagre and barren existence, emotionally so impoverished that we can only be called half alive."

> The author tells of an understaffed orphanage, which housed 97 babies. The attendants had no time for play, comforting or cuddling. Within two years, 34 children had died and another 21 were quite neurotic. The denial of love had taken a terrible toll.

Love means more, of course, than physical love between a man and a woman. It includes friendship, tolerance, sacrifice, empathy, good deeds, and friendly words.

Love is the only game with two players, where both win—the giver and the getter. Unfortunately, most of us give little, but would like to get much.

If you knew that you had only 24 hours to live, would you wreak vengeance on your enemies, pray for eternal life, confess some great guilt, or drink yourself into a stupor?

None of these, probably. More likely you would seek out a parent, a mate, a child and free those tender imprisoned words of love.

Why wait? Why be an emotional miser? Tell people you like them, you love them, you value their friendship—by words, by reassuring pats, by handclasps, by thoughtful acts and affectionate glances. Not once, but again, and again, and yet again—these are the shining gossamer of the heart's immortal craving for oneness.

The Talmud contains this gem of wisdom: "Man is strong, but fears cast him down. Fear is strong but sleep overcomes it. Sleep is strong, but death is stronger. But loving kindness survives death."

FAITH AND WORSHIP

The highest power of your personality is spirituality, stemming from an unshakable, a basic, faith in some higher being. Although we know that there is such a power as spirituality, we understand it inadequately, and are often reluctant to talk about it.

Some ruthless individuals achieve material success with little or no recourse to spirituality, but often pay the piper in neuroticism. Others, despite limited material success, achieve a glowing spiritual adjustment to life.

Belief in a divine power is the zenith of faith, but there are other kinds. You need faith in yourself, that you will be equal to your problems, will do right by others, that you will have courage when needed and compassion when indicated. This kind of faith is firmly rooted in your self-image.

With such faith in yourself, you will develop faith in others— that they, too, will want to do the right thing, will show integrity when put to the test. Nor will you be dissuaded by a few instances which seem to belie your faith.

It is comforting to belong, to know that you have the psychological support of others. Psychologists call it the "herd instinct." Here again to get support you must give it.

Your faith in God transcends creed or your particular form of worship. However, never mistake the form for the substance; observing rituals does not automatically confer upon you a basic faith in God.

Is your faith strong enough that you believe a higher spiritual Being is concerned with your welfare? That everything works out for the best in the long run? That communication with Him through spoken prayer or unspoken thoughts can revitalize your life?

Faith needs practice. When courage or compassion is needed,

162

practice it. When belief in your fellow man is needed, believe. When troubles ensnare you, tell yourself that you have the strength to overcome them. You must voyage these strange seas alone.

HAPPINESS IS—

Happiness, then, is all the things we've talked about, and more. But primarily it is your reaction to the events of life. Emotional maturity helps, as do work, play, love and faith. The accomplishment of strongly felt aims, progress, service to others, giving of yourself, self-respect, harmony in the home, serenity, good health—these all have one by-product in common: happiness.

Figure 17 may help you understand yourself better. It is hoped it will make you realize that there's already quite a flock of bluebirds hovering over your life. Don't fill out this scale when you're up on cloud 9, or down in the dumps. Do it when you're at a point of emotional stability, and evaluate your average mood over the last three months.

Study low-rated factors. Want to do anything about them?

FIGURE 17
Happindex scale

For each factor below, check the phrase which comes closest to the way you feel about it. Base your opinion on the last three months.

Factor	Feeling				
Home relationships	Hostility	Considerable dissension	Some bickering	Peaceful	Loving
Work relationships	I fight my job every day	At times I don't like it	It's O.K., I guess	It's quite satisfying	I'm inspired by my work
Financial security	I feel very insecure	Very doubtful	At times I wonder	Looks pretty good	I feel quite secure
Physical activity	Practically none	Some mild activity	I get it in spurts	I get enough	I get regular exercise
Recreation	Virtually none	Too busy for much of it	Occasionally I get some	I get enough	I enjoy lots of it
Recognition from others	They seem to dislike me	I'm ignored	I get by all right	I'm praised occasionally	I'm well liked
Group participation	None. I hate groups	I intend to join one or two	I belong to a few	I take part in several	I love to be with various groups
Creative expression	I feel thwarted in this	I don't care about it	My hobby gives me this	I have several outlets	I find it in my work
Mental peace	I'm in mental chaos	I'm all stirred up	A few things disturb me	Things turn out all right	I'm mentally serene
Spirituality	That's for the birds	Not much I guess	Occasional spiritual uplift	I feel spiritual assurance	I feel very close to God

14

Your three worst enemies

Each decade, the percentage of the population suffering mental breakdowns increases, along with psychosomatically induced diseases. If, as the psychiatrists say, we live in a balance between love and aggression, the evidence among "civilized" nations is that the scales are being tipped in favor of aggression.

NEUROTICISM—THREE KINDS

Failure to handle life's problems in a mature manner leads to neurotic habit patterns. There are three principal ways of reacting to problems or obstacles: (1) aggression, (2) retreat, and (3) standing still.

Faced with some threat, we try to size it up before selecting one of these three reactions. Contemplating some accomplishment of likely benefit, we decide whether to go after it, not to tackle it, or to defer any decision. Whether we are reacting (to danger, for example) or acting (for some hoped-for benefit), we will probably weigh the three possible courses of action.

Under aggression, we attack the opposition, summoning emotion power to mobilize our resources—physical or mental. Under retreat, we try to avoid, get around, or run away from the problem or danger. Emotion power is involved here, too.

Standing still can take many guises: defending your ground, standing pat, pretending the problem doesn't exist, deferring to a later date, refusing to decide, getting more information. These, too, stir emotions, mostly unpleasant.

Aggression which succeeds brings satisfaction and, shortly, emotional peace. Failure can lead to emotional exhaustion, hence physical exhaustion.

Retreat which succeeds can bring calmness, but may later arouse feelings of fear or guilt. If retreat fails, it can mean turmoil and disaster.

Standing still can be mildly satisfying, but if it represents prolonged indecision, it can tear you apart.

Any one of the three ways to meet a problem may be right for any given situation. But if invariably you follow one only, you will become neurotic. So think of all three avenues as open to you, size up each obstacle and choose the one avenue best designed to enhance your progress and happiness.

THE UNHOLY TRINITY

You've heard of the Holy Trinity—but did you know that in human affairs there is also an *unholy* trinity: hate, fear, and guilt.

Much of the unhappiness in our lives stems from various manifestations of hate, fear and guilt. In this chapter, we'll put these three negative emotions under our microscope.

In the previous chapter, we noted two situations which cause unhappiness: You want something, but fail to get it, or you are forced to do something you don't want to do.

Either of these situations is calculated to arouse some combination of anger (hate), fear (of failure or consequences, for example), or guilt (what you did, or failed to do).

HATE WEARS MANY CLOAKS

Hate is the most powerful of the Unholy Trinity. Here are some of its guises:

Resentment	Jealousy	Impatience	Prejudice
Hostility	Cruelty	Sarcasm	Setting traps
Revenge	Ridicule	Heated argument	Resisting
Physical attack	Sadism	Intolerance	authority
Envy	Practical jokes	Xenophobia	Harsh words

Obviously these manifestations run the gamut from mild hate, such as playing practical jokes, to violent hate, as in physical attack. Most hatred builds up over a considerable period of time, frequently culminating in a heart attack, apoplexy, physical violence, or other catastrophe.

> Some Japanese employers have set aside a room in which there is a dummy hanging from the ceiling. When an employee is fed up with his boss he can go into this room and work off his hatred by pounding the dummy. Then he returns to his job, some of his hostility released.

It's quite a job to get rid of hate. You can't snip out a hate snit like an appendix, nor do as your friends admonish and just "forget it." Hates are like termites in that they work in the darkness of your subconsciousness. There they multiply, gnaw away at the foundations of your personality. Like termites, however, they can't stand searching light. So if you *really* want to get rid of a hate (most folks don't), you should examine it carefully. Where did it originate? Of what possible value is it to you? What situations aggravate it? What is it doing to you? Next, substitute some positive *action* each time it asserts itself. At the outset this action need not be concerned with the person you dislike, but can be directed toward some one who is sick, or discouraged, or in need of help, advice, or other assistance. When you reach the point that you can tender these aids to the object of your former hatred, the termites will be dead.

FEAR—THE SILENT ERODER

Like hate, fear wears many masks. It is a built-in protection, to give you an opportunity to size up your enemies or obstacles. However, it must be controlled lest it spread rapidly like a prairie fire, and become terror.

> Some years ago, Orson Welles put on a fake broadcast about an invasion from Mars. It was so realistically done that many thousands of listeners panicked. Some packed a few belongings and fled their homes. Telephone lines were clogged. In a few communities the police and national guard were alerted. The whole hoax illustrates how quickly fear can take possession, even become contagious.

Some fears are of external things, most are internally generated; a few are sheer imagination. Nevertheless when you're ensnared in any one of them, it seems vividly real. Ripples of anxiety can join up to become tides of fear.

Whatever the cause, real or fancied, fear can set off the body's "alarm reaction" with its consequent train of emotional turmoil. When the danger is past, or the fear conquered, emotional balance is restored.

> When I first had to speak before a group, I trembled at the thought as well as the actuality. After years of public speaking, the fear disappeared. Addressing a group then seemed as natural as face-to-face communication with one individual.

This little story reveals the key to overcoming most self-generated fears. Fear of public speaking? Join a debating group. Fear of water? Learn to swim. Fear of losing your job? Take a pertinent course of study. Fear of the big boss? Offer suggestions for improvement. Fear of death? Read up on diet, exercise, and health.

There is some affirmative, confidence-building action to overcome each one of your fears. Not just ideas or hopes, but *action.* You are not alone in fearing, all mankind suffers with you. Some conquer it by chopping their big fears into manageable pieces and handling them one at a time.

OVERCOME YOUR LONELINESS

You are lonely; all those other folks seem to enjoy a gay, carefree social whirl. You're probably mistaken. Loneliness is prevalent, especially in cities.

Mates of successful executives feel neglected. Married couples wish they'd be invited to homes of acquaintances. Spinsters and bachelors put up a bold façade. Old folks introvert, feel abandoned.

There are three kinds of loneliness:

1. The indifference of crowds, such as is experienced by those who live in a large apartment complex, but find companionship with few of their neighbors.
2. The solitude of circumstance—the night watchman, the forest ranger, the church sexton, the long-distance truck driver.
3. Self-inflicted loneliness, sometimes resulting from real or fancied slights, or from differences in cultural or financial status.

168

Loneliness exists within some homes. Husbands and wives go
their separate ways; children find comfort with their own age
group only; married children, once out of the nest, ignore their
parents. Uneducated parents, who have struggled to provide education for their children, feel a widening cultural gap, often retreat
into loneliness.

To overcome loneliness, you need repeated friendly face-to-face
contact with the same people. Likely, they're lonely too—hoping
that someone will seek them out. Here are eight ways to cure your
loneliness:

1. Maintain or renew contact with your family by telephone,
    letters, cards at holidays, visits, invitations, or gifts.
2. Help someone who is lonelier than you. Maybe that someone
    lives in your neighborhood, or has the apartment across the hall
    from you.
3. Get acquaintances to talk about themselves—their activities,
    hopes, problems, family.
4. Join a group with interests similar to yours. Take an active part
    in it.
5. Attach yourself to some strong leader who espouses a cause
    you believe in. You will draw strength from him even as the
    satellite earth draws heat from the sun.
6. Ride a hobby, preferably one where others have formed a club
    around it. Examples: stamps, coins, antiques, minerals.
7. Exercise your creative talents. Take instruction in drawing,
    painting, ceramics, handicraft. Many in the class are lonely, too.
8. Join a physically active group—hiking, tennis, bowling, square
    dancing. You'll derive psychological, as well as physical benefit.

If you grope in the dark valley of loneliness, it is because you
choose it.

YOU, TOO, CAN CONQUER GRIEF

Grief over the loss of a loved one is a tragic burden to bear. It is
usually accompanied by resentment—Why did God do this to me?—
and guilt—Why didn't I give more love while he, or she, was alive?

Most bereaved persons find solace in daily routine until they
come upon some small reminder—the high school graduation pic-

ture, the humorous birthday card, the fleeting glimpse of someone reminiscent of the departed loved one. "I can get through the day," the grieved one says, "but the nights—!"

Part of your grief is not only sorrow for the fate of the loved one but also self-pity for your own loss of love and companionship. If you don't want to introvert, you need to find new human warmth, and the best way to find it is to give it.

To surmount your grief, you must first face up to your irretrievable loss. Hang on to the happy recollections, let the unhappy ones recede. Perhaps you can find surcease in prayer and religion.

Activity *in new directions* will push unhappy memories aside, as will substituting concern for the needs of others.

There is another side to the coin of grief: how *you* can best help someone in sorrow. Here are some helpful hints:

Don't hesitate to talk about the one who has passed away.

Let the sorrowing one talk, even if repetitiously.

Accept tears, a normal expression, for grief released becomes the instrument of ultimate healing.

No small talk in an attempt to divert the bereaved one. Plain silence would be better.

Be empathetic, but avoid the don't-take-it-so-hard approach.

Keep in touch by phone, letter, or visit, from time to time. Do things together.

Helped the bereaved one to take on new interests and activities.

Remember that a friend in time of trouble is a twice-friend.

NEEDLESS WORRY

Mark Twain once said, "I've suffered a great many catastrophes in my life. Most of them never happened."

Needless worry can drain your energies much the same as genuine stressors. A mother worries when her child rides off, wobbly, on his first bicycle—yet she knows she must let him do it. A married couple worries about having money to pay the mortgage company. A child worries about his parents' reaction to his report card. Rationally, each one of them knows that worrying won't alter the situation.

Preparation and good planning can avoid much worry. The child practices riding his bicycle in the backyard. The couple saves a fixed sum each week. The child studies his lessons so that school marks will be high.

Most worries are minor, trivial. Some people let these dominate their everyday thoughts. You can avoid needless worry by:

1. Planning for the long pull. Then the minor setbacks become less important--so why worry about them?
2. Face the *worst possible* outcome. How serious would it be? Could you survive it?
3. Prepare for action about the immediate problem. Then,
4. Take affirmative action.

Worries, like nagging insects, will often fly out an open window when you start to move toward them.

BURDENS OF GUILT

Guilt results from actions (or thoughts) which contravene standards; or from failure to do something you feel you should have done. Either type of guilt disturbs your self-image and may manifest itself in depressiveness, martyrdom to duty, secretiveness or oversensitiveness.

Here are some typical causes of guilt feelings: dishonesty, disloyalty, immorality, violation of laws, violation of mores, unethical conduct, deceit, unjust criticism of others, unworthy thoughts, lack of achievement, indolence, dereliction of duty, unfulfilled promises, failure to meet your own, or family standards, neglect of loved ones, failure to accept responsibility, vain regrets as to loved ones.

Guilt is a cancer of memory; long endured, it consumes vitality. To lighten its burden on your soul, here are some things you can do:

1. Face it, quit trying to deny it, or make excuses for yourself. Admit it. You did it. What's past is past. If you blundered, you are not the first.
2. Examine the standard by which you judged yourself guilty. Social standards of conduct change. Maybe you contravened the standards of your parents, not of your contemporaries.

3. Confess it to the injured person, if it will not make the situation worse; or to the spiritual leader of your church; or to God in prayer. Unburden your soul.
4. Look forward, not backward. So order your life that you will not repeat the mistake. Build new personality habits to this end. Thus you transmute the dross of guilt to the gold of good.

Maybe it's not too late to return stolen property, take back the unjust words, atone for sin, take further education, seize that opportunity, change the direction of your life.

It is important that you lessen, or divest yourself entirely of guilt burdens by harboring thoughts and building living habits which accord with your self-image.

Learn from your mistakes. Resolve never to repeat them.

NEGATIVE AND POSITIVE EMOTION POWER

In Chapter 12 we talked about stressors, alarm reactions, ductless glands, hormones and emotion power. We saw that a stressor sets off the alarm reaction which prepares the body for fight or flight. When the threat has passed, or the obstacle is conquered, quieting hormones offset the exciter hormones to restore balance, peace, contentment.

In Chapter 13, we reviewed the four conditions which yield happiness or unhappiness. In this chapter we are considering the three major causes of unhappiness—hate, fear and guilt.

The three members of the unholy trinity are interrelated. You can hate a parent and feel guilty about it. You can be afraid of someone and be ashamed of yourself (guilt). You can feel guilty about some misdemeanor, and be afraid you will be found out. The negative emotion power from one will prolong and reinforce another.

FORGIVENESS

Diseased minds never forget; healthy minds forgive.

General Robert E. Lee, when questioned, praised an officer who had made critical remarks about him. When reminded of this fact, Lee remarked, "You asked my opinion of him, not his opinion of me."

Your unwillingness to forgive someone who has hurt you snips the line of communication between the two of you. Frequently, stubborn pride enters the gap, becomes a strong barrier.

Forgiveness is probably the greatest balm *to yourself* that you can find. So learn to forgive. It will make you feel good. Your real or fancied hurts will dissipate.

DOMINANT EMOTIONS IN YOUR LIFE

Figure 18 gives you an opportunity to consider the dominant emotions in your life. To get the greatest benefit, follow these instructions:

FIGURE 18
Self-analysis of emotions

Below are 60 items of emotional traits. Read them over once, to become familiar with the areas they cover. On a separate sheet of paper, enter the number-letters of *exactly* 30 items which are characteristic of you. Do it now, before completing this chapter.

1D	I'm very impatient	31D	Resent life's injustices
2E	Evade responsibility when I can	32E	Afraid of some tame animals
3F	Failed in most of my ambitions	33F	Neglected my parents
4A	Have faith in people	34A	I have great patience
5B	My job is secure	35B	Optimistic about future health
6C	I'm an honest person	36C	I don't consciously hurt anyone
7D	Often use sarcasm	37D	Afraid I have a "short fuse"
8E	Crowds frighten me	38E	Feel insecure in my job
9F	Have some sex guilt	39F	Doubt the value of prayer
10A	Envy virtually no one	40A	Rarely if ever use sarcasm
11B	Equal to life's problems	41B	Parents were loving
12C	Made good work progress	42C	Achieved many of my goals
13D	People can't be trusted	43D	Folks say I'm intolerant
14E	Inadequate; feel inferior	44E	Some people intimidate me
15F	Wasted educational opportunities	45F	Have done some dishonest things
16A	Most things work for the best	46A	Rarely play "practical jokes"
17B	Do not fear death	47B	Accept responsibility
18C	Prayer brings me comfort	48C	Thoughtful of my parents
19D	Play mean tricks on people	49D	Envy many people
20E	Health outlook is poor	50E	Thought of death scares me
21F	Have been unjust to someone	51F	Made little work progress
22A	Readily forgive others	52A	I take frustration in stride
23B	Not afraid of anyone	53B	Like most tame animals
24C	Have met parents' expectations	54C	Seized educational opportunities
25D	Brood over injustices to me	55D	Hold grudges against some folks
26E	Easily swayed by others	56E	Parents hostile toward me
27F	Ignore others' misfortunes	57F	Failed my parents' hopes for me
28A	Tolerate other races or religions	58A	Throw off feelings of injustice
29B	Form my own firm opinions	59B	Enjoy crowds
30C	No guilt as to sex	60C	Help others less fortunate

1. Since some of your self-ratings are very private, do not mark on Figure 18. Instead, use a separate piece of paper to record your self-rating.
2. Select *exactly* 30 items which describe the way you act or feel. On your paper, record the number-letter of each item you select. Consider your present status, not the past. If you're not sure, list it anyway, even if you go back and cross it off.
3. At the end of this chapter is a method of scoring and interpreting your results. If you now read on, you will bias your findings—so do the selection of 30 applicable items *now,* recording their number-letter on your paper, and set the paper aside until you have finished reading this chapter.

DESTROY YOUR THREE ENEMIES

Destroy your three enemies- -before they destroy you. We have previously mentioned a study by Dr. Raymond Pearl, of Johns Hopkins University, who undertook to determine the causes of longevity. After years of research he concluded that peace of mind seemed to be the one characteristic possessed by most of the old-sters. Their hard-hitting, go-getting friends, their timid and worri-some relatives, their ambitious, driving bosses were amoldering in their graves, while these serene old folks lived on. But the unholy trinity—hate, fear, guilt—can destroy your serenity. When any of them are present within you, peace of mind is impossible. You've got to root them out, like thieves- -as indeed they are, for they steal your greatest treasure, contentment. "I do so want to find peace of mind," you say. "How can I acquire it?" Here's how to rid your life of the unholy trinity:

First, you must want to, so much that you will change your reactions to hurts, frustrations—and your own negative thoughts.

Second, keep telling yourself that you are going to do the positive things, and think the positive thoughts advocated in this chapter.

Pep yourself up each morning. Do it all day long: I will be patient. I will be strong. I'll be friendly. I'll help. I have the courage to meet this situation. Nothing daunts me. I'll make restitution for a wrong. I'll forgive someone who has hurt me. My guilts have no place in my present life.

So you will build inner strength.

Third, build personality habits, just as surely as you build the hundreds of other habits you use each day—dressing, preparing a meal, tipping your hat, running a lathe, typing a letter, using a telephone. Typical personality habits are saying thank you, greeting persons you know, praising when it is due, listening attentively. There are negative personality habits too: interrupting, overtalkativeness, sarcasm, temper displays, fussing over trifles, ridiculing, criticism. These negative traits harm you, tear you down, generally indicate a feeling of insecurity on your part.

Note that the prescription to get rid of all three of the unholy trinity contains a common ingredient: Do something. Confess, for guilt. Contra-action for fear. Substitute action, for hate. When such actions are habits of your personality, you will react in the new ways, not as before. Then the trinity will be gone from your life, you will be a greater person, contentment will be yours. You will be one of the lucky ones whose cup runneth over with mental peace.

INTERPRETATION OF FIGURE 18

Previously, you have entered 30 (no more, no fewer) number-letters on a sheet of paper. Ignore the numbers, pay attention to the letters only. Count and enter here the totals of:

D items____(they refer to hate)

E items____(they refer to fear)

F items____(they refer to guilt)

Total____(destructive emotions)

Here's a guide to interpreting these figures:

1. If your total is 15 or more, you are probably trapped in emotional turmoil, need to realign your attitudes and actions. It is *important*. Reread this chapter every week until you've conquered your negative emotions.
2. More than 4 *D* items suggest that you are consuming yourself with hate.

3. More than 4 *E* items suggest that you are afraid to face life, need to assume greater courage.

4. More than 4 *F* items suggest that you are carrying burdens of guilt which you need to shake off.

If you have low scores on these items, I'm happy for you. You're in balance emotionally. Bully for you!

15

What do you *really* want?

The emphasis in this chapter's title is on the word "really." Many high school seniors say they want to be doctors, lawyers or executives, but for most of them these wishes are not much different from those of young children who want to be firemen or policemen.

Want has to be strong, motivating to action, enduring if it is to achieve your goals. Aims, goals, hopes, ambitions are fine—but they're just idle dreams until you set to work to realize them. You won't pitch in because you're inspired; rather you'll feel inspired because you've started something you want to do.

WANTS SHOULD BE SPECIFIC

Success is getting something you strongly want. This simple definition immediately turns the focus on what do you want? *Strongly* want!

To be success-galvanizing, a want must be specific:

Not "marriage" but "marriage to Jennie—or Johnny—Jones."

Not "a high income" but "$50,000 per year."

Not "help mankind" but "a clergyman," a "psychiatrist," or a "teacher."

Not "a scientist" but "a chemist," an "engineer" or a "sociologist."

Get the idea? By having a specific want you can set a specific goal—and experience the joy of success when you achieve it.

Obviously you can have a lot of successes in your life: education, career, family, finance, fame, recognition, security, health. The other side of this coin is that you can suffer a lot of failures.

Sometimes the immediate, specific goal is less than some larger, ultimate goal. I knew a man who wanted, who *really* wanted, to become a doctor. His parents couldn't afford medical school, but he put himself through a course in pharmacy while working in a drugstore. After five years running his own drugstore, he saved enough to complete his education, is today a successful physician.

> I am reminded of a huge, lazy mountaineer in Tennessee who sat in a chair whittling most of the day. A small neighbor said to him, "If'n I was as big as you'n, I'd go up to yonder mountain and catch me a big bear with my bare hands, so's I could feed my family." The huge one kept on whittling as he slowly drawled, "They is little bears up there, too."

Don't hesitate to hitch your wagon to a *nearby* star. When you get there, you can more easily take off for a more distant one.

By achieving a succession of increasingly difficult goals, you get the joy of repeated success, and mounting confidence in your ability to attain the ultimate goal.

Some of the goalposts on the way may seem minor, unimportant. Remember that the world is more enriched by an excellent auto mechanic than by a faulty auto designer. But if you don't have your eye on the *distant* star, you'll probably hitch your wagon to some nearby hitching post.

SIX BASIC WANTS

Underlying important goals are important wants. Psychologists and sociologists have proposed various classifications of human needs.

Maslow (see Chapter 6 and Figure 12) has suggested five levels, running from physiological needs up to self-actualization. He has further pointed out that when most needs at one level have been satisfied, an individual begins to set goals at higher levels. These two concepts (five levels; reaching for higher levels) are useful in understanding the insatiable demands of people.

After many years of puzzlement as to wants, I evolved the six-fold classification mentioned earlier: dominance, submissiveness, creativeness, possessiveness, gregariousness, and homing. In my seminars, I use a simple memory device for these six: *Don't Send Carelessly Packed Goods Home.* Let us consider some subdivisions of the six basic wants:

Dominance—physical domination, intellectual superiority, social status, honors, assertiveness, display, competitiveness, persistence, power-seeking, danger-seeking, authority, leadership, fighting, pioneering, desire for freedom from restraint, curiosity, exploration.

Submissiveness—obeying rules or laws, conforming to a group, accepting customs, following a leader, assisting, imitating, sacrificing, losing in competition, acceptance, giving in, security, self-abasement, religiousness, maintaining the status quo.

Creativeness—handwork, music, art, literature, original research, designing, constructing, repairing, manipulating, solving puzzles.

Possessiveness—owning and caring for property, land, clothing, objects of art, collecting stamps, stocks and bonds, cataloguing possessions.

Gregariousness—desire for acceptance by the group, joining, comfort with the group, giving and getting social approval, sympathy given or received, teamwork, team spirit, play.

Homing—a catchall term for sex drive, love and mating, security and protection of family, homemaking.

This classification excludes needs for food, water, air and physical activity. In our country, these are so available that we accept them as part of everyday life.

ACHIEVEMENT

Under hypnosis, a subject *believes* something and acts accordingly. If he is told that the room temperature is zero, he will shiver. He reacts, not to the fact, but to his belief.

So it is with many of your fears, phobias and apprehensions. You fight them, or flee from them even if there is no substance to them.

Suppose you can develop some positive, benign, success-building beliefs. Not just mouthed words, but real, honest-to-goodness *beliefs*. Will you act accordingly?

Most people equate money with happiness. Union members strike for a large wage increase. The senior executive hops to another post, lured by a huge salary inducement. Yet neither union member nor high status executive captures the elusive bluebird.

Until life's testing brings revelation, cowards can masquerade as heroes, lies as truth, intelligence as composure, notoriety as importance, intention as accomplishment and wealth as success. The trials of life are the assayer's acid which identifies gold from dross.

Maybe you have a strong yen for honors and recognition. These are pleasing when they come your way, but the greatest honor is not in receiving them, but in *deserving* to receive them.

WHAT *DO* YOU WANT?

Here's a checklist of many things people can want:

Health
Strong physique
Resistance to disease
Abounding energy
Excellence in sports
Good health in old age
Relaxation
Play; recreation
Time for contemplation

Mental Development
High school diploma
College diploma
Postgraduate study
Additional training
Better memory
Larger vocabulary
Better creativity

Social Development
Many friends
Acceptance by a
　certain group
Overcome shyness
Public speaking
Leadership
Important status
Power over others
Recognition; honors
Enduring fame
Participation

Career
Better job in present line
Different line of work
Greater income
Great wealth
More career satisfaction
More responsibility
High proficiency

Family Life
Marriage
Own a home
Better living quarters
Children
More peace in home
Accomplishments
More appreciation
A hobby
More affection
Financial security
Valuable possessions
More recreation

Emotional Stability
Control temper
Freedom from worry; peace
Avoid loneliness
Overcome guilt
Greater faith in people
Greater faith in God
Self-respect

Probably you want most of these things, may already have many. On a separate sheet of paper, list five of them which you would like to achieve in the near future. Be specific where possible —not "valuable possessions" but "a 30-foot motor boat"; not "play" but "square dancing."

How much do you want the things you have listed? Strong desire can fuel your travels over a long, rough and tortuous road. However, since everything has its price, how much time, energy, thought, or money are you willing to spend or sacrifice to get them? And don't be afraid of setbacks—you must risk bee stings if you want to gather honey.

After each of the five items on your list, write what you will do to get it—also when!

Are you sufficiently motivated by the prospect of accomplishment that you'll get started right away? Or will you just use bad luck as a whipping boy? Fate can indeed be cruel—especially the kind you ask for by poor choices, omissions, "someday" intentions, and lethargy (a polite word for laziness).

Perhaps the storms of life have tossed you about so much that you're ready to give up, to just seek shelter. Remember that a rainbow accompanies many storms, if you will just look for it. It may not be obvious from where you stand; you may have to stick your neck out to see it.

Good luck and ill fate are two sides of the same coin; don't risk coin tossing for *your* success.

SPECIALIZED WANTS

Because of your individual situation, you may have certain specialized wants. For example, if you're a technically trained employee, you may want challenge in your field, a chance to acquire advanced technical knowledge, someone to listen to your suggestions, and leeway to solve technical problems on your own.

Suppose you're a territory salesman. You'd like to plan your calls, have some discretion as to credit and discounts, latitude as to which items to push, help from the home office in getting information on prospects, a voice in how you will be compensated.

Virtually all specific wants are individualized manifestations of the six basic wants set forth earlier in this chapter.

WANTS CHANGE

Wants change with age, and with accomplishment. Consider a 20-year-old unmarried man or woman, a 30-year-old man with a wife and 3 children, a 40-year-old man with a wife and 3 adolescents, a 50-year-old couple with 3 married children, a 60-year-old widow, living alone, a 70-year-old widow, living with a married daughter, an 80-year-old widow in a retirement home.

These seven stages in a life suggest changing wants with age. There are other influences which can enter in. For example, you can be dominant in one situation, submissive in another. James M. Barrie wrote a play called *The Admirable Crichton,* which tells of a British family, shipwrecked on a lonely island; the humble butler thereupon takes command to save them all. You may be gregarious at noon, but not at midnight. (I know all about this one.) You may spend 40 years collecting rare oil paintings (possessiveness), then give the whole collection to an art gallery (dominance, display, need for approval).

We are just such bundles of seeming inconsistencies, unless you recall, "*D*on't *S*end *C*arelessly *P*acked *G*oods *H*ome."

YOUR AMBITIONS

Figure 19 offers another approach to understanding your goals. Fill it out thoughtfully; if you don't want to mark it for prying eyes to see, use a separate sheet of paper. Write out the ten rating items; after each one enter the numerical score (2 to 10) value of your self-rating. Study your low-rated items for actions you may want to take.

YOUR ACCOMPLISHMENTS

Figure 20 is a sequel to Figure 19. In Figure 20 you appraise your development in ten areas. Here again, if you wish, you can record your ratings on a separate sheet of paper.

Some of the items in Figure 20 may have no significance to you, hence a low rating may mean little. You alone can make this judgment.

182

FIGURE 19
Your ambitions

In each of the ten lines below, check the block which comes closest to your self-appraisal. If you can't decide between two blocks, check the narrow space between them. Be honest, but not harsh with yourself!

Factor	2	3	4	5	6	7	8	9	10
Financial progress	Practically no financial progress		Progress has been very slow		I enjoy normal growth in earnings		My earnings are high but savings low		I'm earning and saving a great deal
Possessions	I really don't care about worldly goods		I'm careless about my possessions		They're O.K. for my station in life		I like nice things		I own many valuable possessions
Status	It means nothing to me		I've never had any important status		I've achieved a little		I'm still climbing the status ladder		I secretly glory in my status
Recognition	I've never had any recognition		I can recall one only		They haven't amounted to much		I get some occasionally		I'm thrilled at recognition I've received
Security	I have no job or money security		I feel very insecure		Sometimes I doubt that I have security		I believe I have pretty good security		I am quite security-confident
Family cooperation	There is hostility in family members		We tolerate one another that's all		In emergencies we pull together		We work together well all the time		We help one another achieve goals
Creativity	I have no creative ambitions		I'm afraid my attempts would fail		I'd like to do something but don't know how		I'm learning how to be creative		I create new things or new ideas
Goals	I'm afraid I don't have any		To avoid poverty and dependence		Security throughout life		Wealth and possessions		Peace of mind. Happiness
Social service	I'm lucky if I can take care of myself		Nobody asks me, so I don't help		I give to charity— that's enough		I help others from time to time		I experience joy in doing for others
Perseverance	I'm easily discouraged		I flit from project to project		I think I'm average in persistence		I'm more persevering than most people		I never give up in pursuing my ambitions

FIGURE 20
Your accomplishments

In each of the ten lines below, check the block which comes closest to your self-appraisal. If you can't decide between two blocks, check the narrow space between them. Be honest, but not harsh with yourself!

Factor	2	3	4	5	6	7	8	9	10
Career progress	Actually I've fallen behind		I've made no career progress		My progress has been very minor		I've had pretty good advancement		I have a history of rapid progress
Manual skills	I detest any kind of manual work		I avoid it when I can		I make minor repairs only		I enjoy doing mechanical work		I'm highly skilled in manual work
Office practice	I dislike and avoid office work		I do it poorly and reluctantly		I get by		I do it well and thoroughly		I have wide experience in this field
Social sciences	I dislike social science subjects		I have no interest in them		Sometimes I read about them in the newspapers		I subscribe to a social science magazine		My education is in the social sciences
Speech	People say that I mumble		My speech is very hesitant		I use "and-uh" and "but-uh" a lot		My words flow smoothly		I speak distinctly without hesitation
Economics	I know nothing about this subject		I have a dim idea about it		I read about causes of inflation		I'm interested in economic problems		I'm a student of current economic theories
Physical sciences	I dislike physical science subjects		I have no interest in them		Sometimes I read about them in the newspaper		I subscribe to a science magazine		My education is in the physical sciences
Arts	I have no ability in artistic matters		Art leaves me cold		I feel neutral about it		I enjoy art in several forms		I create in some form of art
Sports	I have never participated		I no longer have any interest in sports		I follow results in the news media		I watch TV sports with interest		I am, or have been, very active in sports
Use of time	I'm a time waster		My time is poorly organized		I take time as the need arises		I usually plan how I'll spend my time		I make most careful use of my time

184

Here's an idea which may interest you. A few years ago, I used some of these self-analysis scales in a seminar of young men in business. Several years later, one of them wrote me, "I photocopied your ten self-analysis scales in duplicate, filled one set out as your seminar unfolded. Recently, I became curious as to whether I had made any progress, so I filled out the second set. Results are attached."

I compared the originals with the recent scales, was pleased to note improved self-ratings in 70 of the 100 items covered by the 10 scales. Maybe you, too, would like to check up on your own development. A year from now?

REWARDS OF THE SUMMIT

Would you like to climb from the soothing valley of doing-nothingness to the dangerous peaks of leadership? It's a rocky path, strewn with hardships and disappointments, but there are rewards awaiting you at the summit.

High places are lonely places, and strong people often must stand alone as they make important decisions or plan the group effort. Leader and follower may hear the same drummer, but only the leader can point the direction of the march.

Virtually all worthwhile endeavors of mankind need leaders—people who have the required knowledge and who will devote their time and energy to planning and directing others for the accomplishment of the group purpose.

Followers will intuitively recognize your leadership potential. It is far better to let others lift you on to their shoulders with acclaim than to have you climb on to their shoulders with disdain, as do the egocentric power-seekers.

In an earlier book I wrote, "The seeming miracle which elevates the few to high places . . . is really a congeries of powers exercised, talents developed, courage asserted and aims followed, as a mariner his compass."

This chapter may have made you feel a bit uncomfortable. Perhaps it has asked you to poke around the wants in the shadowy recesses of your subconscious. Don't tell me, or anybody else, what you found there.

Tell yourself.

16

Be master of your emotions

Previously we have noted that the unholy trinity—hate, fear, and guilt—causes most of your unhappiness, while appearing in many guises and admixtures. Depression is one outward manifestation of the unholy trinity at work.

Depression Danger Signals

The National Association for Mental Health has released ten "Depression Danger Signals" in an effort to bring about a better understanding of the most common and perhaps the oldest of mental disorders.

The Association emphasizes that many of these signals can be predictable reactions to disappointments, loss, or stress. It is only when they persist or are aggravated by one's lack of ability to "bounce back" that the onset of depression should be considered. Then one should seek professional help. Several of these symptoms are usually present. They are interconnected so that one feeling or mood may lead to another.

The ten symptoms to be on the lookout for are:

1. A general feeling of hopelessness and despair that pervades all of one's life.
2. An inability to concentrate, making reading, writing, and conversation difficult.
3. Change, usually a decrease, in physical activities, such as eating, sleeping, and sexual activity. Early morning awakening is the most common sleep disturbance.

> ### Depression Danger Signals—*continued*
>
> 4. A loss of self-esteem which brings on continual questioning of one's worth.
> 5. Withdrawal from others to avoid possible rejection, even though there may be no basis for the fear. Withdrawal brings on loneliness and reinforces the feeling of lack of worth.
> 6. Threats or attempts to commit suicide which is seen as a way out of a hostile environment and a belief that one's life is hopeless and worthless. (About 1 in 200 depressed persons actually commit suicide.)
> 7. Hypersensitivity to words and actions of others and general irritability.
> 8. Misdirected anger and difficulty in handling most feelings. The perceived feeling of worthlessness produces general anger directed toward oneself.
> 9. Guilt feelings when a person assumes he is wrong or responsible for the unhappiness of others.
> 10. Extreme dependency on others, which brings on feelings of helplessness and then additional inner-directed anger.
>
> Depression is caused by a reaction to a change in one's life. The reaction may manifest itself as a change in body chemistry and the connection to the life event may be obscure. Other times the depression may be *obviously* connected to a change in one's life.

Source: National Association for Mental Health.

These signs are, of course, manifestations of Selye's *stress.* Usually they run a course, then you make some kind of adjustment and the signs lessen in intensity, disappear entirely, or even can be converted to positive attitudes. Looking back, for instance, the discouragement or defeat you suffered several years ago may now be revealed as merely a milestone on your progress road.

Depression has some positive aspects. It permits surcease from a problem that hasn't been solved and avoidance of new or different demands. Some psychiatrists believe that depression is the adult equivalent of a child's crying: it seeks and gets attention. Moreover, they say, depression-disturbed people frequently resort to creativity (painting, writing, inventiveness) and produce health-restoring things of beauty or value.

As with all negative emotional states, if depression is long endured, however, great personality (and ultimately physiological) changes result.

Sometimes a simple change of diet, living habits, environment, or schedule will eliminate a repeated source of irritation. Experiment with this idea for some of your irritants.

EMOTIONAL MATURITY

At one time in my life, I reported to an executive who was a physical dynamo, a mental giant, a social lion—and an emotional infant. Waves of negative emotion swept over him like a storm-tossed sea. I couldn't help admiring his tremendous capacity—nor fearing his uncontrollable wrath. He was emotionally immature. He ceased browbeating subordinates at the age of 46—permanently.

Per contra, we all know people who are considerate of others, meet adversity eye to eye, are calm when others are excited, exude a contagious serenity. They are emotionally mature folks who have learned to control their dynamite-emotions.

> Speaking of self-control calls to mind the story of the father who was pushing a baby carriage in which was a lusty, howling infant. "Take it easy, Johnny," the father said quietly. "No need to get excited."
>
> A woman passerby congratulated him. "You certainly know how to speak to Johnny—calmly and gently."
>
> The man said, "His name's Harold. I'm Johnny."

Emotionally mature people can laugh at themselves and their foibles. They admit their blunders or inconsistencies and accept blame before someone beats them to it. As the years roll by, when they're no longer young enough to be sure of everything, they become more tolerant. Instead of seeing each issue as either black or white, they realize that often there is a large area which is gray. When others call them heroes or geniuses, they are humble—they know their own weaknesses and limitations. They have learned that empathy means more than sympathy.

Folks trust, respect, and lean on those who are emotionally mature.

RATE YOURSELF

In previous chapters we have mentioned so many negative and positive emotional traits that it isn't necessary to repeat them here. Instead, Figure 21, "Are You Emotionally Mature?," gives you an opportunity to appraise yourself in this regard. Read it over carefully before doing the rating.

Be honest with yourself—there's no fun cheating at solitaire!

POSITIVE EMOTION EXCITERS

Positive emotions can be conjured up by the magic of satisfying specifics of your six basic wants. (Remember $DSCPGH$?) Recall that happiness results from:

Having a strong want and satisfying it.

Not being forced to do something you don't want to do.

Recall, too, the Maslow thesis that when wants are met at one level, you begin to itch for satisfactions at higher levels.

These three are large principles in understanding human behavior, including your own. Stated more briefly, they are:

1. Six basic wants account for most behavior.
2. Satisfaction results when a want is satisfied, or a nonfelt want is not forced.
3. Wants, satisfied, stir wants at still higher levels.

If you would be above scurrying humanity, eyes focused solely on survival, apply these three principles to yourself, by

1. Identifying your specific wants at this stage of your life, in the six basic areas.
2. Determining what preparation *and actions* are indicated to satisfy each one.
3. Considering what higher level wants you should look forward to, after successfully completing Nos. 1 and 2 above.

These actions on your part will provide you with galvanizing positive emotion power which will prevent or easily overcome most negatives which will assail you. A psychologist once remarked to me, "The best way to avoid being overcome by thugs is to keep some strong bodyguards handy."

FIGURE 21
Are you emotionally mature?

In each of the ten lines below, check the block which comes closest to your self-appraisal. If you can't decide between two blocks, check the narrow space between them. Be honest, but not harsh with yourself!

Factor	2	3	4	5	6	7	8	9	10
Control under pressure	I become unnerved		I rely on someone else		I manage to get through it		I face up to pressures		Nothing seems to phase me
Reactions to criticism	I get very angry when I'm criticized		I argue with my critics		Secretly I resent it but don't argue		I listen with an open mind		I analyze it for truth or benefit
Tolerance	I am intolerant of many groups		I have a pet peeve about one group		I can't stand certain individuals		I try to understand everyone		I have great compassion for all peoples
Freedom from envy	I envy a great many individuals		I envy wealthy people principally		Some folks don't deserve their good luck		I'm pleased with my own accomplishments		Folks are entitled to what they achieve
Humility	I cover up inadequacy by boasting		Sometimes I brag a bit		I don't "hide my light under a bushel"		My accomplishments speak for themselves		I never "blow my own horn"
Work satisfaction	I hate my job		I'd like to do something else		I dislike some parts of my job		My work is pretty enjoyable		I'm wrapped up in my work
Moodiness	I doubt that my life is worthwhile		I'm usually in low spirits		I swing from high to low, low to high		I'm usually in a pretty good mood		I'm cheerful, not moody, most of the time
Decisiveness	I'm torn with indecision		I defer rather than decide		I decide when I have to		I consult others before deciding		I have no trouble deciding for myself
Relaxation	I'm tense most of the time		I have an ulcer or spastic colon		At times I can't seem to relax		I rarely feel muscular tension		I'm really a very relaxed person
Spirituality	I don't believe there is a God		I'm skeptical about a "Benign Creator"		God is sure not concerned about me		I'm genuinely religious		I have faith in God and mankind

190

USE THE POWER OF AUTOSUGGESTION

Ever notice how easily you can talk yourself into a foul mood? Someone criticizes you unjustly, or deceives you, or breaks a promise, or cheats you, or—you name it.

You're full of resentment. Again and again, in your mind's eye, you roll over the unfair situation. You'd like to strike out at someone, at something. You're caught in the throes of hate.

Maybe you're threatened with physical harm, loss of a loved one, shameful exposure, financial disaster, insecurity, loss of status. Fear has a headlock on your emotions.

Perhaps it's guilt that keeps nagging at you. You should have done this, you're sorry you did that.

Whether it's hate, fear or guilt, you feel terrible all over. Your muscles are tight; appetite gone; that old ulcer is kicking up; you're irritable; feel tired; need a stiff drink; would like to lie down, except that you know you couldn't sleep.

Who among us has never been caught in the tentacles of such negative autosuggestion? Yet none of us can really afford such emotional binges.

You can reverse the process by *positive* autosuggestion:

Consciously relax your large muscles—shoulders, back, arms, legs, abdomen. Review Chapter 3 for the benefits of this practice.

Resurrect some pleasant memories.

Think thoughts opposite to what is bothering you—you're equal to the problem; your opponent has many good traits; there are two sides to every question; you'll not repeat the offense, and so forth.

Sing, whistle, listen to music, turn on the TV.

Take on some muscular activity—walk, swim, exercise, paint.

Finally, forgive the person who seemingly has hurt you. When you can reach this point, your emotional snit is over.

FAMILY LIFE

A fond memory of my own childhood is a dog of "uncertain ancestry" who lived to the ripe old age of 15. I can still recall the pall that settled over our household when he died.

Someone to care for? A dog, yes. Why not each family member?

Emotional control is especially important in family life.

Cowardly child abuse is on the increase. Harshness alienates the growing child. Between husband and wife, the ambrosia of love sours to gall and wormwood, with the final dregs quaffed in the divorce court. Brothers and sisters mistreat one another. Sociologist Richard J. Gelles reported to the American Association for the Advancement of Science that "Violence between family members is at least as typical as love."

When you're out of emotional control, the very proximity of a family member provides someone on whom you can vent your spleen, like a child who kicks a door.

On guard! That's the stuff which makes for indifference, hostility, divorce, revenge, family schisms--and vain regrets.

Try forgiveness, gentle words, caresses and love. They will work magic.

COURAGE

Where do you find courage? It is easy for me to say, "Buck up. Face your weaknesses, your problems, your enemies."

"But," you ask, "how do I find that courage?"

Your principal opponents are yourself or other people.

In previous chapters we talked about your self-image. If you see yourself as a frightened mouse, you have no way of calling up your reserves; at the moment you have no courage.

Do other people intimidate you? Here's a situation you can do something about and at the same time build some self-confidence. You undoubtedly have knowledge or skill in certain matters; when they are under consideration, speak up. Take your stand, even though others disagree; you have a right to your opinion, a right to be heard. Have the courage of your convictions, for if you merely walk in the paths trod by others you will never discover the mysteries which abound in the underbrush.

Actually you learn more in this life from those who dispute your passage than from those who readily let you pass.

You can learn to assert yourself without becoming hostile or aggressive. Assertiveness means that you tell clearly how you feel, what you want, or what you are going to do.

No pussyfooting, no maybes, no halfway measures. No anger, no loud tone, no punishing words.

If you are timid about some upcoming situation, rehearse in advance what you will say, and just how forcefully you will say it—but be sure that what you will say is what you want to say. With this preparation, courage will come to your defense like a knight in shining armor.

If you are suddenly confronted with an unexpected demand, you can always say, "Give me some time to think it over."

If you learn to assert yourself, folks may not always agree with you—but they will respect you.

Finally, avoid such an adamant stand that you leave no room for possible compromise. You might not be in possession of all the facts. You might even be wrong!

Historians tell us that whole civilizations have crumbled when the people became soft, surrendered their independence to self-serving leaders, docilely accepted the hammer blows of fate, lost the will to struggle on. Do these devastating phrases describe you?

Cowardice cringes, courage acts. Do something, don't just think something. Say it. Write it. Take action, even if it is just training so that you can later move with certainty. Ally yourself with others who want the same things as you. Work for a cause. Plan for it. Lead it.

As you do these things, it may never occur to you that you are exhibiting courage—but you are.

STAYING POWER

Temporary success can sometimes be achieved by a lunge of effort, but permanent success requires staying power.

It is not only fame or financial success that requires staying power. Emotional maturity does also. Many houses are built to withstand strong winds, but perhaps not hurricanes. If your emotional reaction patterns (i.e., ways of meeting life's problems) are mature and ingrained, you'll outlast the hurricanes and become that much more confident of your ability to overcome your emotional devils.

There is a prayer which contains a sound philosophy, "Lord, grant me the serenity to accept the things I cannot change; the courage to change the things I can; and the wisdom to know the difference."

MEDITATION

True meditation counteracts stress—feelings of hate, fear, guilt—which sometimes surfaces as indecision, time pressures, responsibilities, obligations, insecurity, worry about the future, divided loyalties and other emotional imbalances. Meditation can yield an inner peace which is more to be desired than a blustery front which makes others tremble.

As we have said, transcendental meditation (TM) has caught the popular fancy. Its proponents believe that it helps students find self-awareness, define their goals and learn better.

It is estimated that TM has almost a million followers, largely stemming from the teachings of a Hindu, Maharishi Mahesh Yogi. Its adherents include doctors, lawyers, businessmen, TV entertainers, athletes, industrial workers, housewives, students and many other classifications.

In a previous chapter we brought out that TM is a method for getting rid of negative emotions and finding a haven of peace. The state of meditating is one of deep rest, but not of sleep, for you are completely alert.

If you take instruction you are assigned a word called a secret "mantra" which, in meditating, you reiterate in your mind. In essence, you put yourself into a state of mental and physical relaxation. Some followers say they get a pulsating feeling in the head and a tingling in the arms and legs. Afterwards they feel loose, fresh, happy, and confident.

Critics assert that the whole movement has become sadly commercialized. Members of Indian sects say that TM as practiced in America demeans the legitimate practice of meditation, the beloved child of silence.

Dr. Herbert Benson, a Harvard cardiologist, showed that TM resulted in decreased heartbeat, respiration, and metabolism. He also concluded that what he calls the "relaxation response" can be achieved by sincere meditation. The main elements seem to be a quiet environment, with no interruptions; a comfortable position, achieving relaxed muscles, eyes closed; a receptive, passive attitude; mental repetition of a single, meaningless syllable or word as you breathe out; continuing for 20 minutes at each session; staying with it until it's an established part of your life.

Even a few minutes in which you count your blessings will prove helpful. I call this practice my "lucky me" relaxation. Sometimes, when stressed, I merely recall some pleasant memories.

Some—and I'm one—can derive great relaxation from soothing music. On the other hand, most symphonic music stimulates me. So find out which music lulls, which inspires you, and seek it when the need arises. Maybe your "thing" is not music, but poetry, painting, sculpture, who-done-its, historical novels, or masterpieces of literature.

You're never too old to use some form of meditation.

BIOFEEDBACK

Until recent years it was believed that you have no direct control over functions governed by your sympathetic (autonomous) nervous system. As we have said, experiments are suggesting otherwise—biofeedback.

For example, migraine headache sufferers are learning how to raise the temperature of their hands 10 or 15 degrees, so decreasing the flow of blood to other parts of the body, including the brain. Presto—the headache eases or disappears.

Heart patients have been trained to smooth out irregularities in rhythm. Subjects with high blood pressure have learned to lower it. Brain waves have been altered. Paralyzed muscles have been restored to use. Pain has been eased.

> In normal sensory-motor coordination, a basketball player, learning to shoot fouls, practices thousands of times. He gets the muscular feel of the ball as it leaves his hand, sees how close he comes to the basket— *feedback* of sensory impressions. Gradually, he makes the sensory-motor corrections until he possesses high accuracy.

Biofeedback techniques supply the equivalent of sensory-motor feedback, by use of electrodes attached at points of the body where control is being sought. The electrodes detect, then electronic equipment amplifies, minute changes of skin temperature, blood pressure, heart, muscles, converting them to clicks, shrill sounds or light flashes.

Typically the patient is seated in a comfortable soundproof

room, the electrodes connected to the area he is trying to control. The equipment gives off audible clicks. He learns that he can increase and decrease their rate or intensity by concentrated thought. For example, an allergy patient may first be told to think of ragweed pollen, which increases the clicking, then of pollen free ocean air, which subdues it. After a few training sessions, some patients learn to control their respective conditions without the aid of any equipment.

Considerable success has been attained in the treatment of asthma, migraine headaches, muscular tension, paralysis, epilepsy, back pain, various neuromuscular problems—and childbirth.

Conscientious researchers decry the fact that charlatans are making unproven claims for biofeedback equipment. The techniques are still experimental, but extremely promising. They are not panaceas for any and all ailments; they frequently alleviate but do not utterly cure. At best they are useful adjuncts to the arsenal of healing agents which the field of medicine has at its command.

AT THE END OF YOUR ROPE?

Feeling desperate? Everything you've tried gone wrong? You don't know what to do next? Where to turn?

In a few communities there is a "crisis line" you can call; it has different names in different localities. If you feel pressures mounting—and mounting—and *mounting,* find out if there is a crisis line in your area. Then, should you reach the breaking point some time, you have something, someone to lean on.

However, there is a surer approach. The military call it indoctrination—deciding what you will do in the event of various contingencies. Having decided in advance, you have something to fall back on when you really and truly need it.

There is a still better way. You can't foresee catastrophe or plan for sudden emergencies. These can take you by surprise, throw you off balance, put you into an emotional tailspin. What then?

Faith is the answer. Confidence in yourself, your fellow man, your God. You can't do any better than this—if your faith is strong enough, you will win even if an outside observer thinks that you lost.

FAITH

In discussing courage, we mentioned the importance of faith in yourself. Oftentimes, an inspiring idea sparks a leap of faith which becomes a burning belief in some ultimate outcome. Such was the case with Thomas Edison, who worked for five unrewarding years to develop the electric light bulb. In most great achievements undying faith precedes glorious victory.

Faith in others is equally dynamic. Without it, man would soon revert to his prehistoric caves. With it, he can live in a loving family, a peaceful community, an orderly society—despite aberrations by a recreant few. Faith in a higher being helps in developing the brotherhood of man.

A snowflake. A hurricane. An acorn. Lightning. A newborn baby. A sunrise. Healing tissue. Spring flowers. Can you doubt a God?

Faith is the epoxy which glues our lives together. It is revealed in religions, in prayer, in self-confidence, in brotherhood, and in service to others.

Most people feel shy talking about their faith in God, yet they readily find common ground when they do so.

We are prone to think of faith healers and psychic healers as possibly charlatans. No doubt some are. Others are working with physicians and scientists in an endeavor to understand the well-authenticated miracles which sometimes occur. Since many ailments are psychosomatic in origin, it makes sense to believe that properly induced thought can reverse the process which brought on the illness.

Much the same can be said for *genuine* prayer, the spoken or thought manifestation of faith. Even rote or ritual prayer can have value if the supplicant has faith that it will—the "magic of believing."

17

Put it all together

There comes a time in every life—and in every book—when the parts should fit together.

> Last summer I watched a stonemason build an arched walkway over a small stream. At first, a pile of uninteresting looking stones. Under his skillful hand a beautiful arch slowly took shape, a large keystone in the center.

Let this book be your keystone so that each stone you lay in your personal development will support others.

THE MID-LIFE CRISIS

In *The Divine Comedy* Dante has this sentence: "Midway on the path of life, I found myself in a dark woods." Many men and women make a similar discovery in their lives, frequently around the age of 35 to 40.

Social scientists believe that the typical individual evolves through various stages, somewhat as follows:

In the 20s—seeking the satisfying, specific career, often by means of job-hopping.

About the age of 30—settling into a career channel; setting job, status, and money goals for himself.

Five or ten years later, may feel trapped, so makes a significant job change or perhaps goes into business on own.

At 40, feels at the midpoint. Assesses accomplishments against goals; may suffer guilt at partial failure. The threat of society's cult of youth begins to haunt. Detects some physical signs of aging— thinning hair, glasses, overweight. Alcohol and younger persons become more attractive. Spouse may be experiencing counterpart pressures.

Frequently, depression ensues. Life no longer unfolds as a glorious adventure.

The brilliant Swiss psychiatrist, C. G. Jung, noting these phenomena, gave us three useful observations:

1. Nature intends that all phases of life shall have meaning, but not necessarily the same meaning for each phase.
2. If the second half of life is to provide serenity, it must include a belief in some form of life after death.
3. The second half may need goals and standards different from the first half.

If you are at, or beyond mid-life, heed these three guideposts. The business of the mature is internal wisdom. Aging should be serene; it can be joyous.

IMPROVE YOUR ENVIRONMENT—IT'S IMPORTANT

So far, we have largely talked about *you*. But you do not exist in a vacuum. Your total environment shapes you all the time. In this chapter we shall consider your physical, career, and social environments; in the next and final chapter, the political and economic milieu under which you function—and attempt to lift the curtain for a peek at the future.

In Chapter 2 we touched upon lighting and noise as possible sources of danger to eyesight and hearing. You should consider both home and work situations to be certain that you are not injuring these two important senses.

The air you breathe—is it laden with dust, pollen, tobacco smoke or harmful fumes? People crowded into a small room can soon vitiate the atmosphere, substituting carbon dioxide for life-giving oxygen.

Temperature and humidity are interrelated. Warm air can absorb more moisture than cold air. High humidity makes you feel uncomfortable because the surrounding air cannot evaporate perspiration from your body fast enough. At the other extreme arid air absorbs moisture from your eyes, nose, mouth, throat, skin.

Most heated homes and offices have too little moisture content in the air. In general, you should:

1. Try to keep the air temperature between 64° and 68° Fahrenheit.
2. Add moisture to artificially-heated air.
3. In hot weather, use air conditioning or electric fans.

Distractions interfere with concentration, and place unnecessary adaptive demands upon you. Noise and incorrect lighting are the obvious sources, but there are others: uncomfortable chair, wrong height of working surface, vibrations, unexpected jolts, moving objects, vivid colors.

Orderliness as to objects in daily use adds to good environment. Cluttered desks, work places, and rooms cause unnecessary expenditure of energy in finding things or in moving about. Good housekeeping may well add a few percentage points to your total effectiveness.

Efficient lighting, pleasing color combinations, subdued but harmonious sounds, rhythm, pleasing odors, and orderliness are the opposite of distractions. They soothe the senses, provide an environment conducive to effective work and yield a peaceful mental attitude.

WORK ENVIRONMENT

Many adults spend a considerable portion of their lives in a work environment—typically an office or shop. Laws are increasingly forcing employers to make work places safer and healthier.

However, some employers are voluntarily making them more pleasing esthetically. No more drab walls, small dirty windows, insufficient lighting, foot-aching concrete floors, dust- and fume-laden atmosphere. Instead these far-sighted employers provide pleasing wall and machine coloring; large windows that look out upon colorful plantings; no forbidding partitions between employees and supervisors; pleasing, glare-free illumination; sound-absorbing ceilings; wooden or resilient flooring for work places; air filters or conditioning; and cheerful, sanitary eating facilities.

FIGURE 22
How about your environment

In each of the ten lines below, check the block which comes closest to your self-appraisal. If you can't decide between two blocks, check the narrow space between them. Be honest, but not harsh with yourself!

Factor	2	3	4	5	6	7	8	9	10
Lighting	Poor lighting 8 or more hours per day		Poor lighting 3 to 7 hours per day		Lighting is mostly acceptable		I live and work under good lighting		Excellent lighting most of the time
Atmosphere	Polluted with dust		Polluted with smoke, fumes or bad odors		Sometimes good, sometimes bad		Mostly air conditioned		I breathe pure natural air
Distractions	Many noise, visual or other distractions		They're quite annoying at times		I've had to get used to them		I can concentrate despite distractions		I don't have to endure distractions
Employer	Worst company I ever worked for		I'm going to quit as soon as I can		No better, no worse than other employers		Many good features		Great company, excellent boss
Fellow workers	They're contemptible		They're unfriendly		I manage to tolerate them		They're mostly O.K.		They're friendly and helpful
City or locality	I dislike living where I do		I'd prefer another part of the country		Present locality is O.K.		It's better than most others		I live in a great section of our country
Neighborhood	I'm fearful where I live		I dislike my neighbors		It's the best I can afford		Most of my neighbors are quite friendly		It's a great community
Home environment	I'm part of frequent angry bickering		I live in a hostile environment		Occasional family squabbles		Family members are friendly		Love is all around me
Social companions	None. I'm a lone wolf		I rely on one person only for companionship		They're really just acquaintances		I have a few good friends		I have many great friends
Betterment activities	Mostly radio or television		Mostly newspapers		I read books and magazines		I'm mastering subjects by reading		I'm taking educational courses

Such a work environment allays tensions and gives employees a feeling that they are more than mere numbers on the payroll.

Figure 22 permits you to evaluate ten significant aspects of your physical environment.

What actions will you take to improve some of the low-rated items?

SEEK OUT THE RIGHT PEOPLE

If your physical environment is important, your psychological environment is even more so. An employer can provide you with ideal working conditions, but you won't be happy in them if you're not adjusted to your fellow workers. Your home may display affluence, even culture, but not affection among family members. Your church may offer wise sermons, soothing ritual, prayerful worship, and spiritual music without thrilling your soul.

Psychologists say that you can improve your emotional stability by avoiding people who lack it—folks whose attitudes are bleak, and whose comments destructive. It is wise to shun people who are hypercritical, envious, soured on life. They generate a powerful suction which is slowly whirlpooling them down to tragedy or oblivion. However, you need to seek the positive, not just avoid the negative.

Stop right now to think—who are the people who will provide the emotional climate in which you can properly pursue your various life objectives?

You must deserve such people; otherwise they may be shying away from you.

Your present associates may now be compatible, but a drag on your advancement or happiness. You may have adopted their speech or recreation habits, thereby precluding your acceptance by others whose eyes are lifted to higher horizons. I am not advocating that you dump your friends to become a social climber. I am suggesting that you consider whether the people with whom you associate help or hinder you in pursuit of your life's goals.

Success in business offers an obvious example. On a number of occasions I have participated in sessions where candidates for some important promotion were being discussed: experience, education, ability to get along with others, and emotional maturity were the prime considerations. But, if two or more candidates could meet these criteria, the social contacts and cultural progress often became the deciding factors. Most of the time, you never know why you weren't promoted, or were not accepted by some desirable group.

Much the same is true in all social acceptance: whom you know counts. However, if you continually rely on "pull," you may lack a lot of push.

Whether it's in the home, place of work, church or club, avoid spending much time with people in a pressure-cooker atmosphere.

A few individuals are so well organized that they can take on numerous obligations—often by delegating much of the legwork to others. Of them, people say, "If you want something done, give it to a busy man." However, most folks shirk responsibility, so that willing horses soon get overworked.

Weigh each request to take on some added obligation by using five criteria:

1. Is it important?
2. Is it consonant with my objectives?
3. Will it interfere with other important activities in my life?
4. Will it yield me satisfaction?
5. Will it bring happiness to others?

Your answers may be a mixed bag of yes and no, but they may help you reach a decision.

If you accept, mean it. Don't take it on, then do nothing.

If you reject the possibility, say "No" and mean it, softening your answer with some reasonable explanation that will shut out argument or further pressure. For example: "I know it's a worthy cause, and I wish I could devote the time to it that it deserves. However, I can't because _____. John Jones is both capable and interested. Why don't you ask him?"

BE MISERLY WITH YOUR TIME

Time is the only currency that cannot be counterfeited. If I handed you $8,760, you would give considerable thought to how to spend it. Will you give equal consideration to how you should spend 8,760 hours per year?

Here are some time savers:

1. Have a place for everything, and keep everything in its place. This practice avoids time-wasting searches for needed objects.
2. Carry a memo book, with perforated detachable pages. Write obligations or other notes; tear pages out when obligations are completed; or file pages in a tickler file.
3. Maintain a 12-month–31-day tickler file to bring up deferred subjects for action at the right time.
4. On a monthly wall calendar note future commitments.
5. Each morning plan your hoped-for activities; assign priorities. If planned items are numerous, list them and check off as they are completed.
6. Avoid, or restrict, people who waste your time on trivia. Those who have time to spare frequently seek out someone who hasn't.
7. Eat a light midday meal, without alcohol, so you won't be sleepy in the afternoon.
8. If you supervise others, avoid activities which subordinates could perform.
9. Avoid, or simplify all paper work. File or discard completed items.
10. If yours is a desk job, retain *necessary* current papers in a vertical desk distributor, properly labeled.
11. If yours is a shop bench job, keep tools and accessories in designated locations and close at hand.
12. If you're in territory sales work, plan your calls and allot time for each call.
13. Avoid working on several projects simultaneously, unless you have to wait on one of them.
14. Answer some letters by returning with marginal comments; if important, retain a photocopy.
15. Don't make a habit of taking work home for night and week-end handling.

Father Time travels in one direction only, makes no return trips. So the best use of time is not just to sit on your status quo. Consider, for example, how you use your *spare* time, wherein you have some options. What will you read or do? What groups will you join, or meetings attend? Which individuals will you seek out? Use the time for relaxation or meditation? The cumulative effect of these decisions alters your future.

DRAMATIZE YOURSELF

Learn to present your ideas so that they are emotionally convincing, not merely factually accurate.

Understanding is intellectual; conviction emotional. Showmanship—dramatization—involves the use of emotion-evoking power words; a contributory stage setting; curiosity-stirring suspense; sudden surprise; or participation by the one to be convinced.

If you shrink from the idea of using showmanship in communicating with others, then be content to watch with admiration those actors who don't share your false qualms.

> A tire salesman was endeavoring to sell me his brand. After a brief recital of facts, he handed me a hammer and blunt screwdriver, saying, "If you will drive a hole in this demonstration tire, you will see how thick the tread is." I struck the screwdriver a heavy blow, which didn't make the slightest impression on the tough tread. Then, indeed, I was convinced. He had used showmanship to persuade me.

Plan ahead for difficult situations you will likely encounter, where presentation of facts, plus dramatization by you, should win the day. It's fun!

AGE AND PRODUCTIVITY

Some readers of this book may think, "It's too late for me to change. My life is a burden which I must accept—I'm 40 years old (or 50, or 60, or 70)."

Researchers selected 400 men and women who had made great contributions to mankind over the centuries—statesmen, warriors, philosophers, writers, painters, historians, etc. They secured agreement as to the greatest accomplishment of each person and determined the decade of his life when it had occurred. Sixty-four percent of the greatest achievements of the world were made by persons 60 years of age and older! How old did you say you are?

You're too old, huh? The German poet, Goethe wrote three of his important works after the age of 70. Sir Francis Galton, an English scientist, wrote 5 important works after he was 70, was knighted when he was 87. Painters like Michelangelo, Titian, and

Monet were highly productive as octogenarians. Other examples can be found among composers, statesmen, generals and business leaders.

Your age is not a time of life, it is a state of mind–*your* mind. You can be governor of that state!

The other side of the age question is how young are you? And do you mournfully believe that your best years will be behind you when you hit 60, or 65?

Age is physiological, not chronological. We all know people whose life-clocks are running down at 40, and others whose clocks are ticking away merrily at 70.

Heredity, equable temperament, education and good living habits contribute to longevity. In fact, most of the success-suggestions in this book also make for a long, zestful, and productive life.

MARSHALL YOUR ASSETS

Early on, I said I would try to put together the principal contributors to a successful life. How well I have accomplished this aim for you must be judged by benign changes in your own life. If these have not, or do not come about, then I have failed–but so have you.

On the other hand, if you are now fiercely resolved to do many things here advocated, you should, as this chapter title suggests, put it all together.

FOLLOW THROUGH

The habit of following through is one of the distinguishing characteristics of successful men and women. In almost any sport you can mention the top athlete always carries his movements to a perfect follow through. But the benefits of follow through are not limited to sports. Today–everyday–you have opportunities to follow through, on your job, or at home. Here are two simple rules which will help you acquire this success-packing ability:

1. Define clearly the end result of effort by you, or others.
2. At crucial checkpoints, inspect the work or progress, up to the final completion.

Let's apply these two rules to you. You resolve to take a correspondence study course which has 36 sections. You promise yourself to complete one section a week, come hell or high water. You prepare a schedule which you paste on your bathroom wall, as a reminder of your resolve. As each lesson is completed and mailed, you check it off on your schedule. When you mail off No. 36, and on time, you feel a glow of satisfaction that you have followed through on your self-promise. The certificate of completion which now hangs on your wall is a constant psychic reward that you accomplished something you set out to do.

HOW FOUR MEN "PUT IT TOGETHER"

In closing this chapter, let me tell you about three brothers, who all worked for the same large shipping company. Tom was a clerk, earning $10,000 a year; Dick a section supervisor, earning $20,000 a year; Harry a vice president, earning $60,000 a year. A visitor asked the president how three men, brought up under the same home influence could vary so much in earning power.

> The president pressed a button, and Tom appeared. "Please go down to the dock and see if our ship is ready to sail," the president asked him. In a few minutes Tom returned to report affirmatively.
> Then the president brought Dick into his office with the same request. A half hour later he told the president, "She's ready to sail, but the clearance papers weren't filled out properly. They're in good shape now."
> Finally, the president gave $60,000 Harry the same request. He didn't return for several hours, then reported, "The cargo was so stowed that the ship was listing to the starboard. I called back all the stevedores and their foreman, made them load it right. Sorry it took so long, but I stayed there to make sure."
> When Harry had left, the visitor said in amazement, "How did you know the ship was loaded improperly, and how did you know those brothers would react as they did?"
> The chief executive chuckled a bit then said, "Maybe that's why I'm president."

This little story illustrates different degrees of self-development and follow through as exhibited by four men in much the same environment. Note that Harry said, "I stayed there to make sure."

If you bring together all your powers in your circumstance, which one of these four men will you be like?

In marshalling your assets, review the various self-analysis scales you have filled out throughout this book. In light of your greater understanding of yourself, you may wish to revise some of your ratings up or down. The object of this review is to get a composite picture of yourself.

Repeatedly throughout this book, I have talked about your improvement in terms of what you should *know, do* and *be.* Resulting from marshalling your assets, you should now be able to write out some resolves under these three captions. This action will be one way for you to gauge just how serious you are about improving yourself.

You can use this book as a training guide, if you wish. Keep it on your bedside table, or near your favorite chair. A year from now, see how many self-ratings you could honestly put up a notch or two.

18

Plan your destiny—now!

Success, however you or I define it, seems such an attractive prize—until we see its price tag. Many a would-be doctor has settled for medical lab technician; CPA, for chief clerk; mechanical engineer, for shop foreman.

In Chapter 15, I asked you to determine some specific goals for your life. Now I am suggesting that you either reaffirm or revise those goals, to make sure that they are realistic in light of realism as to your future. Don't be ashamed to set lesser, or more immediate goals. They may prove to be satisfying when achieved--or they may become stepping stones to higher things. If they are genuine goals, they will motivate you to action.

Lacking goals, people drift with the tide. Progress has no reverse gear. Today is fast becoming tomorrow's past--but it is also prelude to the future.

Try to envision your future, rather than to dwell fondly—or ponder regretfully—on your past.

CUMULATIVE EFFECT OF CHOICES

Some folks seem to be born losers, but if you trace their lives over a period of years, you will likely find a succession of bad choices.

None of us makes the right decision every time. But if occasionally you wander into a bypath that leads you to a darkened

208

nowhere, grope your way back to the main highway which goes somewhere. Keep your eyes on that road, for it leads to your chosen goals.

The effect of a sequence of wise decisions is cumulative. They support one another, as the base of a pyramid upholds the next higher layers, up to the apex - your chosen goal.

Choices are presented to you every day, every week, every year. Your criterion for deciding: which one continues to point toward my goals.

Choices present mental conflict, but the absence of such conflict in your life may bring ennui rather than satisfaction. However, a comforting peace can be yours from the assurance that you have the ability to cope with the conflict which is forcing a choice, or which is threatening you.

SELF-DISCIPLINE

Successful people practice self-discipline. Undisciplined persons wreak havoc to society, are unreliable to their companions, hurt their loved ones, and tear themselves apart with the unholy trinity.

Some go through life revealing the adult version of a screaming, tantrum-ridden child—ranting, swearing, blaming, evading, alibiing, lying, criticizing, flailing, hurting. Beware of such neurotic individuals; they leave destruction in their train.

Self-discipline can be manifested in many ways: by holding your tongue when you feel like spewing venom; by relaxing when frustrated; by withholding judgment until you have the facts; by persistence in pursuit of your objectives; by meeting obligations on time; by orderliness; by building numerous living habits which ease the daily struggle and free you for tackling complex problems.

Perseverance is one of the surest manifestations of self-discipline. If it seems futile, heed this story of the cork and the girder.

> This was an experiment to determine whether repeated swinging blows from a thermos bottle cork would have any effect on a half-ton steel girder suspended by a chain.
>
> For 15 minutes, the girder seemed unmovable. Then it began to exhibit a slight vibration in response to each tap of the cork. Ultimately it began a ponderous swaying as though it were the pendulum of a Gargantuan grandfather's clock!

When you feel that you are up against an insoluble problem or a situation too great for your powers, remember that persevering cork.

CAREER OPPORTUNITIES AHEAD

Social scientists believe that in the decade of the 60s, we began to phase out the industrial era and enter the "post-industrial" period, which will present opportunities for those who recognize and adapt to the impending changes. Here are some emerging characteristics:

Probable change	Likely stress or benefit	Opportunities
Less interest in work	Guilt on part of many workers	Reduced competition for promotion
More leisure	Boredom for some; health and relaxation for others	Careers in leisure industries. Time for more education
Reduced accent on wealth	Less competitive tension. Greater gap between have and have-nots	Less competition, if wealth is your goal
Less respect for authority	More crime and breakdown of law and order	Need for socially-minded leaders
Rapid changes in technology	Unemployment; preparing for new careers	Need for persons technically trained
Rise in computer applications	Unemployment; higher productivity	Careers in computer, automated production and communication fields
Continuing inflation	Lower standard of living for many	Economics, finance, investments, politics

Look to the distant horizon for your career opportunity. New jobs are emerging and old ones disappearing so rapidly that most employees under 30 years of age will likely have two or three distinct careers over their lives. Bear in mind that the rewarding joy or punishing aversion from any task is in your mind, not in the work itself.

DAILY LIVING HABITS

Ingrained habits relieve you from making decisions hundreds of times each day. You dress, shave, clean your teeth, drive your car, do repetitive tasks, eat meals at certain times, turn on the TV and go to bed as matters of habit. Little thought is involved. Most things you do throughout the day have been learned; those done repetitively have become habits.

You can build physical, mental, social, and emotional habits. Some are detrimental to your success; for example, smoking cigarettes, excessive drinking of soda pop, guzzling numerous pills, criticizing, gossiping, over-talkativeness, and swearing. Instead of dwelling on negative habits, let's consider some positive living habits which can help you progress:

Physical—Taking daily exercise; maintaining good posture; eating balanced, nutritious meals; getting proper sleep; acquiring skills for work performance.

Mental—Regular use of a dictionary; utilizing various aids to memory; checking your computations; reviewing your reasoning; reading technical journals; planning ahead; consciously thinking positive thoughts and making positive statements.

Social—Saying "please" and "thanks"; according recognitions when due; being prompt for appointments; honoring your word; participating in group efforts; helping others; accepting responsibility; planning for others.

Emotional—Delaying reaction when attacked; asking forgiveness; forgiving the injuring party; analyzing criticism; asserting courage; consciously relaxing muscles; meditating; prayer; reiterating faith in self, others or a higher power; perseverance in the face of discouragement.

Some of these, like "Forgive thine enemy" will not easily become living habits—but practice will get you there!

Good living habits become your character. Character, in turn, plays a prominent part in your ultimate destiny.

Supported by a multitude of superior living habits, you will tower above your fellows like a great oak in a forest of scrub pines.

WHAT TO DO WITH YOUR MONEY

Men far smarter than you or I have puzzled as to how to plan their financial futures. Some have converted their stocks and bonds to cash, which they put into savings accounts, certificates of deposit or commercial paper (i.e., short-term loans to corporations). Some put their faith in gold and common stocks of gold mining companies, pointing out that throughout the history of civilized man, gold has always been a repository of value. Some buy real estate, believing that people will always need shelter, and that land seldom depreciates in value. Others buy up common stocks of industrial companies which sell for low price-earnings ratios, such as five to one.

Two decades ago, I made a graphic comparison of the gross national product (GNP) and stock prices as measured by the Dow Jones industrial average (DJIA). It showed a considerable correlation: as the GNP went up or down, so did the DJIA. Hence, if you believe that the GNP will rise (including inflation) you should believe that stock prices will do likewise.

Authorities suggest these priorities for your income:

1. A reasonable standard of living.
2. Security—savings for some "rainy day"; life insurance for your family.
3. Real estate—house; land.
4. Investments which bring in a return at least equal to inflation.
5. Speculation, if you have anything left over.

Before making decisions on these items, consider the future as seen by both pessimists and optimists.

THE PESSIMISTIC OUTLOOK

Some students of futurism foresee a bleak picture ahead. Their reasoning goes something like this:

1. Inflation is built into our political system, and hence into our economic future. Short remissions will not alter the underlying inflationary trend. Genuine price deflation, such as in previous depressions, is unacceptable to politicians, labor unions, and businessmen.

2. To pay for oil and other raw materials the "have" nations, including our own, have issued fiat (printing press) money at an increasing clip, yielding a false sense of prosperity.

3. Many "have-not" nations, lacking oil or important raw materials for export are being squeezed to the point of desperation. Their rising expectations are being frustrated by harsh reality.

4. Birth rates, worldwide, will bring increasing poverty, starvation, and unemployment to some nations. In certain areas, drought aggravates these conditions.

Barring some dramatic breakthrough in nutrition, large-scale starvation looms. Food experts predict that by 1985 (projected world population: 5 billions) we shall see worldwide shortages of wheat, corn, soybeans, rice, meat, and milk.

Thomas Malthus, a British economist, predicted this situation in 1798, adding that disease, starvation, and wars might keep his prediction from coming true.

Birth control methods have proven inadequate in countries such as India; they have virtually been untried in most countries.

Hungry men are dangerous men; hungry nations are warring nations. Hence the prospect for world peace is a fantasy; survival will be the reality; an atomic holocaust a real possibility.

5. In our own country, minorities are "have-not" groups, suffering from disease, malnutrition, low income, unemployment, and lack of opportunity to remedy these conditions. Hence, crime, rioting, and food looting will increase.

6. Doomsayers believe that we will see a worldwide inflationary binge which will top any past boom, and will be followed by a cataclysmic bust: bank closings; paralyzed commerce and industry; almost worthless securities; and currency depreciation so great that it will take a 100 dollar bill to buy a head of lettuce—but a 25 cent coin will be as valuable!

7. Such drastic upheavals, say the doomsayers, will witness various deviations from present social standards: a decline of traditional religions; internecine strife, even warfare; governmental paternalism, coupled with police state discipline.

8. Some folks are so pessimistic that they advocate converting much of your capital into hard currency (coins and gold); buying a small remote shelter away from cities; stocking it with nonperishable food or raising your own; keeping a machine gun on hand to hold off looting mobs. Obviously, if this scenario comes to pass, civilization as we know it today will be decadent—or a mere memory.

Before you jump off the top of some high building, let's see the optimistic view of the future.

THE OPTIMISTIC VIEW

On numerous occasions over the centuries, men have declared that the world was going to the dogs, couldn't survive much longer. Somehow, it has managed to do so. Change, which sometimes seems so awesome, has not meant destruction.

The futurists foresee a continuing growth in goods and services; a decrease in the work week; more leisure activities; in the U.S., affluence which will lessen interest in the work ethic and financial success.

However, the pragmatic futuists foresee so many international hassles that few are so bold as to predict tolerance, empathy, and the coming of the brotherhood of mankind.

The post-industrial era, which became noticeable in the decade of the '60s, is proving to be the electronic age. Electronic marvels are influencing many phases of our lives: communication, transportation, production, commerce, science, medicine, law, weather forecasting. Applications of electronics in these fields will influence our lives, speeding up the tempo, forcing new adaptations upon us.

I believe that we will make the necessary adjustments in the United States better than in any other nation. I hope that we will be in the forefront in finding the way to personal peace, and in developing compassion for others less fortunate.

OUTSIDE FORCES MAY SHAPE YOUR FUTURE

"Man proposes, but God disposes," says an ancient maxim. Not all your future lies in your hands. You need to be aware of numerous large forces, far beyond your control, which may determine the milieu in which you will live out the remainder of your life. Principally these outside forces are five in number:

1. *Economics*—productivity, labor attitudes, unemployment, management decisions, availability of raw materials, capital, and inflation.
2. *International*—national goals, resources, military power, aggression, trade competitiveness, labor productivity in foreign nations.
3. *Ecology*—air, space, water, use of land, climatic changes, population shifts.

4. *Government,* especially federal—laws, regulatory agencies, welfare, housing, taxation.
5. *Social*—attitudes, mores, goals, education, minorities, equality, and attitudes toward work.

As changes become obvious in these large influences, consider whether they require new knowledge or adaptation on your part, or may otherwise affect your life.

Over the centuries, mankind has sought various sources of reinvigoration. Spanish explorers hoped to find the Fountain of Youth. Our ancestors tried "the baths"—hot springs, redolent with odorous sulfur and containing minerals supposed to cure arthritis. Many religions advocate "retreats," prayer, and meditation. Worshippers find solace or inspiration in the Bible, the Koran, the texts of Brahma, or the teachings of Confucius. Some people find inspiration in the wonders of nature, in great literature, or in overwhelming symphonies. Whatever stirs your soul to love of your fellow man, to good deeds, to noble thoughts or to great accomplishments—partake of that Pierian Spring, the source of inspiration in Greek mythology.

Coming closer to home, maybe this book can be your Pierian Spring, for it endeavors to bring together in one place most of the wisdom of the race as to health, success, and happiness. The author makes no pretense that he is the possessor of all this wisdom; rather he is merely a reporter.

From time to time, and especially when your spirits are dragging, pick up this book and seek answers to your problems or peace for your troubled soul. May it bring you renewed courage is my sincere hope.

HOW DO YOU ENVISION YOUR FUTURE?

We live in a world of contradictions—work hard but do your own thing; live for *now* but save for your old age; cut government spending but increase social benefits. Caught up in this whirlwind of conflicting forces, how can you find *the* way?

The answer lies in self-planning. It is a lonely task, so get all the help you can. If you would scan the road ahead, first light up your imagination as to the kind of future in which you will live. Then let reasoned planning take over. Beware of hunches—the tyranny of sudden impulse must give way to the reign of careful planning. Planning will throw light on the future. Face it, and your shadows will be behind you.

Most economic researches suggest that our country is currently caught up in one of the most profound upheavals in its two-century history. Watch for further changes in social and economic trends. These national and international forces swirl about like a gathering hurricane, but ultimately point in some direction. You can follow the eye of the storm through newspapers, magazines, opinion polls, and television. They can help you touch, if not quite grasp, the future.

Perhaps you have a vague feeling of uneasiness about the future. Since hobgoblins must be faced, if they are to be conquered, let's bring some of your forebodings out into the open. Here are ten questions:

As to your livelihood:
1. Is your income reasonably secure for the next five years?
2. Do you have more than one way by which you could earn a living?
3. From all income sources, could you survive unemployment for six months?

Within the next five years, do you foresee in the United States?
4. Nuclear war?
5. Economic depression?
6. Prolonged food shortages in your community?
7. Riots, especially in cities?
8. Continuing increase in crime?
9. Continuing inflation?
10. Continuing unemployment?

"Yes" to items 1, 2 and 3 suggest self-confidence. "Yes" to the remaining seven items suggest apprehension which you must face.

Neither success nor failure will necessarily be final for you. One success may merely open the door to higher achievement. One failure may merely strengthen your resolve to persevere.

Consider Lawrence Welk, outstanding band leader. When, after 16 years, ABC canceled his show, disaster loomed. Believing that he offered a service which millions wanted, at the age of 68, he had the courage to form his own syndicated network, which now has 40 million viewers. His self-confidence has paid off.

At one time Queen Victoria commented to Gladstone that there were not many good preachers. To this, her prime minister replied, "Madam, there are not many good anything." Herein lies a cue for you—be excellent, not just passable, at something.

The American Dream is still very much alive. It says that you can succeed regardless of family limitations, that you will be judged on what you make of yourself.

In the days of the vanquishing Roman armies, a "lictor" was assigned to each general. In battle, should said general hesitate, it was the duty of said lictor to lash the general, to remind him that his job was to go forward, not to retreat.

Maybe you need a lictor—an encouraging spouse, a long-range goal to be achieved, a coveted prize to be won. You might even use this book as your lictor.

Please don't hide behind the alibi that you're not smart enough. Dr. Catherine Cox Miles, a Yale psychologist, made a study of some of history's outstanding persons. She noted that quite a few had been men of ordinary intelligence, did not tower over their contemporaries in gray matter. Here are some of their names: Lincoln, Cromwell, Drake, Nelson, Emerson, Thackeray, and Napoleon. They succeeded by utilizing traits other than high I.Q.s.

THE WORLD NEEDS LEADERS

You cannot do most of the things advocated in this book without being designated a leader in some of your activities. People will respect you, lean on you for counsel, elevate you, look to you for direction.

The only possible missing ingredient will be your *acceptance* of responsibility.

When the leadership role is offered you, if it is in line with your goals, accept it. It is a great developer of character, planning, patience, perseverance, courage under adversity, new abilities and imagination. In what other situation can you add these valuable traits to your personality?

FIGURE 23
Your leadership ability

In each of the ten lines below, check the block which comes closest to your self-appraisal. If you can't decide between two blocks, check the narrow space between them. Be honest, but not harsh with yourself!

Factor	2	3	4	5	6	7	8	9	10
Acceptance of responsibility	I duck responsibility when I can		I'm an "alibi artist"		I accept it in some matters		I do what's expected of me		I glory in greater responsibility
Planning for others	Let them do their own planning		I really don't know how to do it		I do some planning for others to follow		I set goals for others to reach		I invite joint goal-setting
Training your followers	No one looks to me for leadership		I try to set a good example		I let others learn by trial and error		I utilize an organized program		I train both followers and peers
Use of motivation	I don't believe in manipulating people		I've never consciously tried to motivate		I've read something about it		I try to inspire others		I appeal to the self-interest of others
Persuasiveness	I couldn't be bothered		My words don't seem to change others		I keep pressing my point of view		I have a way with words		I consider how best to persuade
Enthusiasm	I guess I'm a "wet blanket"		I'm not enthused about anything		In a few matters I'm enthusiastic		Frequently I can "light fires"		My enthusiasm is contageous and real
Public speaking	I abhor it		I avoid it when I can		I do it when called upon		I'm convincing when addressing groups		I'm dynamic on the speaker's platform
Showmanship	This is just trickiness		I'm really a very modest person		Secretly I'd like more attention than I get		I enjoy the spotlight		I think up unique actions
Aggressiveness	I am a peaceful person		I don't like contention		I'll fight for what I think is right		I rarely lose sight of my objectives		I persist in getting my way
Courage	I am timid with other people		I avoid conflict when I can		Nobody can push me around		I don't mind an occasional scrap		I'll tackle any problem in human relations

Leadership is scary, for you will be held accountable for success or failure. Leadership is lonely, for decisions must be made at the top. Leadership is rewarding for it brings recognitions, honors, loyalty, and the exhaltation of your spirit which comes from leading a group to some worthy accomplishment. Figure 23 gives you the opportunity to appraise your strengths and weaknesses for this important talent.

YOUR SHOULDER TO THE WHEEL

"These economic, political and international tides are too much for me," you say. "I am just one person in billions." Right?

Wrong. Here are some things you can—nay, you should, do:

1. Follow the precepts of this book as to health, energy, mental development, social activities, and emotion power.
2. Take an active part in your community, church, union, club, parent-teachers' association, or other groups to which you belong.
3. Speak out against injustice, political corruption or other social cancers.
4. Vote in *all* elections.
5. If you're a parent, keep close to your children, with both understanding and discipline; give them sound standards by word and example.
6. If you're in business, join business groups, and make yourself heard.
7. If you're an employee, do your job without griping and do quality work.
8. Keep out of debt, as your contribution to reducing the rate of inflation.
9. The future is a strong wrestler facing you; don't be afraid to grapple it.
10. Keep your faith. Great souls have wills; feeble souls only wishes.

In reading this book you have traveled a difficult path of self-examination. You have covered self-improvement suggestions from scores of sources. The future is up to you.

Index

222